W. H. FINDLAY

Perth & Kinross Libraries

Jacket:

Panorama of the City
The river Tay and the daffodils of the Norie Miller Park.

First Published: 1984
Photolog Press
W. H. Findlay
9 Rosemount Place
Perth, Scotland, PH2 7EH

Second Edition: 1996
Perth & Kinross Libraries

ISBN 0 905452 20 8

Layout: Ernest Greig

Printed by
Cordfall Ltd
0141 332 4640

FOREWORD

I am delighted to be invited to write the Foreword to the second edition of Heritage of Perth. It comes as no surprise that a second edition has been called for, and the addition of an index, a block of colour pages and a hard cover and jacket, along with the revised text, have greatly enhanced what was already a most acceptable publication.

Dr. Findlay has done both Perth and his readers a great service in providing them with such a comprehensive guided tour through the ancient and historic Fair City. It leaves readers eager to go and see for themselves the treasures which are so eloquently described in these pages.

So much of Scotland's history is woven into the story of Perth. It was, after all, the capital city at one point in its history. To many, Perth is a city to pass through on the way north or south; but it would be in the traveller's best interest to stay awhile and explore the Perth of today as well as Perth of yesteryear.

The River Tay provides a superb setting for a rich diversity of our native habitats and species, and there are walks aplenty to delight the rambler with wonderful views of the majestic hills which surround Perth. It was no surprise that Perth and its surroundings won the accolade of having the highest quality of life of any district in Britain.

I fervently believe it is essential that our cultural heritage – both man-made and natural – is preserved for this and future generations, and this book goes a long way to inspire us all to achieve this preservation.

Dr. Findlay has ensured that the Fair City remains in our minds as one of our most delightful places – a gateway not only to the Highlands but to Scotland itself.

Magnus Magnusson, K.B.E.,
Chairman,
Scottish Natural Heritage.

ACKNOWLEDGEMENTS

First and foremost the support and encouragement of Mr F. James Guthrie, District Librarian of the Perth and Kinross District, are warmly acknowledged; also the valuable assistance if his staff in the Local History Department of the Sandeman Library, whose ready help relieved the author of much laborious research.

The help of Mr David Walker of the Historic Buildings Branch of the Scottish Development Department is also gratefully acknowledged. His mature knowledge and experience in the subject of architecture, particularly of historic buildings gave substance and authority which otherwise would have been lacking.

To Miss Rhoda Fothergill, F.S.A. Scotland, local historian, I am greatly indebted for valuable help and for correcting proofs.

My thanks are also due to Mr R.M. Chalmers of Lindsay & Co. Ltd., Printers, for his expertise and help in the creative process of book building.

Finally and perhaps most of all to Marjorie for smoothing the way at all times and in all things; also to Alan and Alison for voicing their support throughout. It is to these three — Marjorie, Alan and Alison that this book is dedicated.

W.H. Findlay, 1984

For this second edition produced by Perth & Kinross Libraries, my grateful thanks to Mr Mike Moir, District Librarian.

WHF, 1996

INTRODUCTION

One man's view of a city's heritage is bound to be a personal one. It will reflect his own interests and those aspects of the civic scene that act upon his own sensitivities.

To most people, including the author, heritage in a civic sense has come to mean buildings. European Architectural Heritage Year comes back to mind with the awareness it engendered of the buildings around us. Whilst the main drift of this work concerns the buildings of Perth as they have appeared in the last 30 years it is not intended that it be solely a "documentary", a record of buildings and nothing more, desirable though such a thing might be. Room has been made for mood and atmosphere, ingredients which to the author are inseparable from heritage as perceived in a city like Perth. A famous film director has said, "Every country has its own mist". Couldn't the claim be made that in Scotland every town has its own mist — its own atmosphere? The River Tay as it passes through Perth settles this tribute upon us on its way to the sea, a rare heritage that changes from day to day and season to season but never palls. But is the appreciation of this available only to those who are accessible to aesthetic impressions? I think not. More people than we realise have this sensitivity and it is for them in particular that Section 8 has been compiled.

Also, the part played by history in shaping heritage cannot be underestimated. The captions to the photographs make frequent reference to this. After all Perth was once a capital city and as such is steeped in history. We may also contemplate that as long ago as the year 1227 a Bishop of Exeter was credited with the following couplet:

"Great Tay, through Perth, through towns, through country flies,
Perth the whole Kingdom with her wealth supplies."

Whatever of heritage Perth may have had then, it certainly appears at least to have had a reputation.

The photographs which form the basic material of this volume and which are drawn from the author's accumulation of over 1,800 taken in the past 30 years are separated into 10 groups each illustrating an aspect of heritage that appeals to the author. The list of buildings of outstanding historical and architectural interest compiled by the Scottish Development Department has provided constant help in the selection process. Section 1 of the book is indeed given over in its entirety to buildings listed in the "A" category. The remaining nine sections are as described in their introductory paragraphs.

To Marjorie, Alan and Alison

The Branklyn Meconopsis

This Variety of the Himalayan Blue Poppy was developed in Perth at The Branklyn Garden by Mr and Mrs John Renton. The garden, now owned and maintained by the National Trust for Scotland, is one of the finest small gardens in the country and is recognised as a valuable heritage of Perth.

All photographs by the author

Festival Finery ▷

The General Accident Assurance Building is here seen bedecked for the Perth Festival of the Arts, an event which takes place annually in the month of May.

This entire building was taken over by the Perth and Kinross District Council in 1984 and now serves as the Council Chambers and Offices.

The Badge of the Black Watch Regiment ▷

The Regiment — properly entitled The Black Watch (Royal Highland) Regiment — has its Regimental Headquarters at BALHOUSIE CASTLE in Perth. The Castle also houses the Regimental Museum and Archives. The regiment is the embodiment of various highland units which were originated after the first Jacobite Rebellion "to keep a watch on the braes". It is not connected with any Highland Clans, the tartan being made to a government design. Recruitment to the regiment is from the areas — Perthshire, Angus and Fife.

"The greatest thing a human soul ever does in this world is to *see* something. . . . to see clearly is poetry, prophecy and religion all in one."

JOHN RUSKIN.

"— leads you to believe a lie
When you see with, not thro', the eye."

WILLIAM BLAKE.

"The Fair Maid of Perth" ▷

Dressed in the period costume of 14th century Perth, this modern Fair Maid is seen here leaving the fictional home of the original Maid Catherine Glover — heroine of Sir Walter Scott's novel which brought fame and fortune to Perth in the early part of the 19th century. A Fair Maid is selected annually for festive occasions.

Civic Window, St John's Kirk ▷

Inaugurated in 1975, this window was the gift of the retiring Town Council of Perth to the Kirk to commemorate the long association of Council with Kirk.

Six basic symbols were used by the artist — Mr HARVEY SALVIN — as a means of highlighting this association, viz. the Crown, the Keys, the Gate, the Ears of Corn, the Fish and the River.

The Crown symbolises kingship and is a reminder that Perth was once the capital city of Scotland. It also symbolises Christ's gift of a Crown of Life.

The Keys and the Gate are symbols of a city safe in the hands of loyal lieges on behalf of a gracious sovereign. They are also symbols of God's Kingdom in Heaven.

The Ears of Corn are symbolic of the farming community in which the town is situated and also of many biblical references to corn and the Bread of Life.

The Fish symbolises the River Tay and Christ Himself. ICHTHUS, the Greek word for fish was used as a code word for Christ. Each letter became an initial — JESUS CHRISTOS THEOU UIOS SOTER — Jesus Christ, Son of God, Saviour.

The River Tay to which Perth owes its early beginnings and continued existence is symbolised as the River of Life.

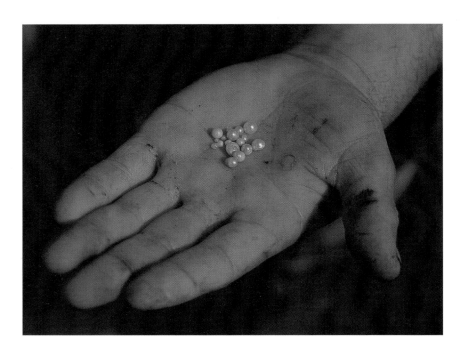

The hand of the pearlfisher
His day's catch, all within the City boundary.

CONTENTS

Page

I   "A" LISTED BUILDINGS   1

II   THE GEORGIAN PERIOD   45

III   PUBLIC BUILDINGS, CHURCHES   59

IV   PRIVATE HOUSES   99

V   CITY WALKABOUT   115

VI   VIEWS AND VISTAS   151

VII   SOME NOOKS AND CRANNIES   163

VIII   AMENITY AND MOOD   185

IX   RIVER ROAD AND RAIL   209

X   RECENT CHANGES   229

I. "A" LISTED BUILDINGS

THE most outstanding buildings in Perth i.e. those listed by the Scottish Development Department in category "A" are brought together in this section. Their prominence is undisputed. They number 14 and are here given pride of place in a section — the first section — to themselves. They are of prime interest in either a historical or architectural sense and it is hoped that their ascendance will become evident on seeing and reading the captions to the photographs. "To see once is a hundred times to hear" quipped the age old mandarin but seeing plus hearing (or reading) is surely better still, and this is our aim here. Let us acknowledge that a good photograph examined in the hand can reveal in seconds more detailed information than minutes of peering from the pavement.

The following buildings are contained in the section. All are listed "A"; but let it be mentioned that certain groups of buildings can be listed in the "A" category although the individual members are "B". They are represented in later sections

St John's Kirk.
Perth Bridge.
The Old Academy and Rose Terrace.
Atholl Crescent, Nos 2-8.
The City Mills; upper and lower.
The County Buildings, Tay Street.
The Old Waterworks, Marshall Place.
King James VI Hospital.
St Leonard's in the Fields Church.
Charlotte Place, corner building.
Barnhill Toll House.
Pitheavlis Castle.
Bank of Scotland, St John's Street.
District Offices, York Place — now the A. K. Bell Library.

St John's Kirk

The Kirk is seen here flooded by the light of a westering sun. Although it could be mistaken for a cathedral or an abbey it is in fact one of few old burghal churches surviving from the middle ages. First mention of it in records was in a charter written some time between 1189 and 1199 but it is accepted that it had been in existence for a considerable time before then — probably since 1127. The Kirk gave its name to the town — St John's Toun — a name in official use for centuries. The building was consecrated by Bishop David de Bernham in 1242 but it was not until the 15th century that the choir was finished — 1448. It is possible, if not probable, that the building suffered damage by fire or warfare in the intervening years — fire in 1244, and warfare during Bruce's wars of independence. The part over the north porch with the crow-stepped gable is known as the Halkerston Tower. This commemorates John Halkerston who was probably Master of Works on the great undertaking. He is known to have been in control at the building of Trinity College Church in Edinburgh some time between 1461 and 1469. In modern times he would be described as an architect.

In 1984, after 60 years, the inroads of time were again showing, calling for extensive repairs to stonework, roof and windows which were carried out.

Provision for an organist and for ringing the bells is mentioned as early 1511. There were three great bells and six smaller ones with additional "music bells". The present carillon is of broad range and of high quality.

The church was one of the largest in the land at a length of 200 feet. Today the vista from the west door (q.v.) looking through to the choir must appear little changed from early days allowing for the many stalls and chapels — there were said to be 40 or more — that cluttered the nave and aisles. These were of course the pre-reformation days which were to come to an abrupt end on 11th May 1559 when John Knox preached his inflammatory sermon against idolatry. The congregation, fired with the desire to "cleanse" the Kirk and other religious buildings swept through them with the speed of a riot leaving destruction in their wake. The fabric of the Kirk survived however and it continues to this day as a people's Kirk under the Presbyterian ordinances of the Church of Scotland. After the first World War, the Kirk, in need of much repair was restored (1923-26) under the able direction of the architect Sir Robert Lorimer. Walls were rebuilt, including the Halkerston Tower, and roofs renewed. Extensive internal alterations and reconstruction were necessary to remove the furnishings of the three churches, into which it had been divided, and bring it back to unity. This great undertaking, designated as a war memorial for the county, attracted popular support. Part of the Sanctuary — a space in the north transept — was set aside and sensitively designed by Sir Robert as a shrine of remembrance for those who gave their lives: 1914-19.

Now, in 1984, after 60 years, the inroads of time are again showing, calling for extensive repairs to stonework, roof and windows. Our heritage in peril.

Architectural Note: Cruciform: five-bay choir with clustered piers, clerestorey and aisles, still with original roof trusses, completed by 1448. Five-bay nave with octagonal piers, aisles with clerestorey, transepts with north-west Halkerston Tower, late 15th century. Central tower with ribbed and leaded broach spire, completed by 1511; 155 feet high: north transept shortened 1823; upper part of Halkerston Tower demolished. Repairs, general and to north and south doorways to choir c. 1827, J. Gillespie Graham; repairs to choir 1893-94, A. Heiton and A. Granger Heiton. New roof and aisles to nave, upper part of Halkerston Tower rebuilt, general restoration and complete refurbishing, Sir Robert Lorimer 1926: Bells, Skelloch, 1400 or earlier, Curfew, Waghevens, 1506. Stained glass: MacNab Window, W. Wilson: east window, titled "Last Supper and Crucifixion", Douglas Strachan 1920: two windows by Marjorie Kemp 1931 and 1933: others by Ballantine, Stephen Adam, Meikle & Son, H. Hendrie and Louis Davis.

3

Some Treasures in the Kirk's Keeping

Silver Gilt Baptismal Basin

The weight and splendour of this handsome dish are matched only by its great antiquity and originality of design. The inscription reads: "For the Kirk of Perth, anno, 1649", but there is clear evidence that it was made 50 years earlier by a goldsmith in Edinburgh called David Gilbert. The overall diameter is 18 inches.

The Offerand Stok of St Eloyi

The Stok, an ancient box made of wood and bound with iron bands, was the strong box of the Craft Guild of Hammermen. Thirteen

4

inches in height and seven inches wide it is over 350 years old. Its two different locks are clearly visible and both keys, each of which having been entrusted to a different member of the guild, were required to open it. In pre-Reformation records it is referred to as "SACT ELOYIS STOK IN YE KIRK". The patron of the hammermen was St Eloyi to whom there was an altar in the Kirk.

The "Mary" Cup

This silver gilt cup, 15 inches in overall height, was made for secular use. (Note the pagan figures of Satyrs on the stem.) It is similar in type to other cups which were fashionable in the late 16th and early 17th centuries. There is convincing evidence that it was made in Nuremberg in the late 16th century. But there is no convincing evidence about the identity of the "Mary" whose name is attached to it. Three Marys are possibles — Mary Stuart, Mary of Guise (mother of Mary Stuart), and Mary of Gueldres (wife of James II) but facts are few in support of any of them. The mystery therefore remains unsolved.

Three other silver gilt cups of equal antiquity and charm are in the Kirk's possession — a Nuremberg cup and two English "Steeple" cups. On display they form a group with the "Mary" cup.

The Candelabrum or Lustre

This hangs in the north transept. It is dated somewhere between 1440 and 1450 and is therefore one of the Kirk's most ancient possessions. Flemish in design and craftsmanship it was perhaps a gift to the Kirk from Queen Mary of Gueldres — wife of James II. Only two other examples are known — one in the Province of Liege and one in Bristol.

The Pews of the City Guilds

On 12th February 1582, the Kirk Session gave permission to the Wrights' Incorporation to erect "decent, comely and honourable" seats in the north transept of the Kirk. This was duly carried out. Their history was respected in the restoration of the church by Sir Robert Lorimer (1923-26) who arranged for the devices of the Guilds to be carved on the new pew ends:

The City Arms

Cordiners (Shoemakers)

Hammermen

Glovers

Wrights

Fleshers

Bakers

Weavers

Tailors

Passion flower carving. Size 10 inches.
The oak pews in both transepts were the gift of the Guildry Incorporation of Perth at the time of the restoration, 1926.

Examples of other carved embellishments on the pews in the transepts

◁ Sleeping lion on a pew arm (on which many a hand has rested). Size: excluding tail, five inches.

Oak leaf and acorn design. Size 10 inches.

Crouching dog. Size: 10 inches.

Crouching ape. Size: 10 inches.

St John's Kirk: The Vista from the Nave

The church was unified at the restoration of 1923-26. Prior to this it had been divided into three by internal walls thus accommodating three separate congregations. Note the central point of worship — the Communion table — under the crossing. This conforms with the ordinances of the Church of Scotland.

The Bells

These bells — 15 in number — were formerly in use in the steeple. The modern carillon, furnished with manual keyboard and automatic player, is one of the finest in the country. It was installed by Gillet and Johnston in 1935. One of the very earliest bells bears the date 1506. The Skelloch bell is 14th century.

Perth Bridge: from The North Inch

Built 1767-1771 by the engineer John Smeaton to replace the ferry which had been in use since 1621 when a flood swept away the "Auld Perth Brig". It was opened to the public on the 31st October 1771. The cost — £26,631 12s. 5¾d. The construction is of red sandstone with nine arches and having a total legnth of 800 feet. The circular openings in the spandrels were designed to reduce the load on the foundations and relieve flood water pressure during exceedingly high spates. They were characteristic of Smeaton and can be seen in his Coldstream Bridge. (John Baxter adopted them in his bridge at Kenmore.) Perth Bridge has stood the test of time and even now, after two centuries, requires very little maintenance. Listed "A".

It was widened in 1869 under the direction of A. D. Stewart; the stone parapets being removed and footpaths on cast iron cantilever brackets were added. The stones from the original parapets were used in the building of the house at No. 2 Tay Street, a few yards distant (q.v.).

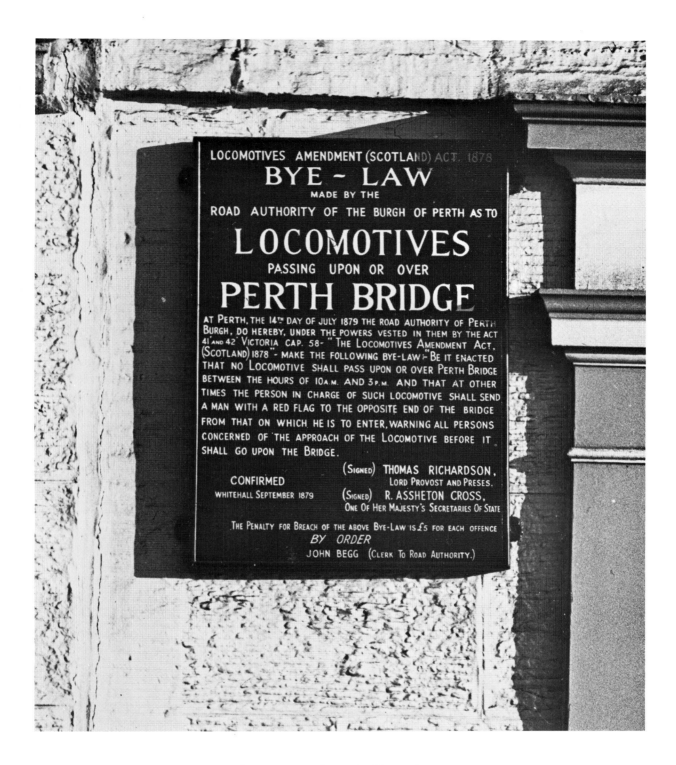

"Locomotives" Bye-law

Situated at the east end of the bridge on the wall near the Bridge Toll (now demolished) this notice has been preserved for those with a thought for the past.

Perth Bridge in evening sunlight

This view was taken from the forefront of the Royal George Hotel where with the help of the light of a low sun the strong lines of the bridge's design and its obvious stability were clearly revealed.

One of two identical plaques beside the pavement on each end of the Bridge

BRIDGE BUILT 1766

WILLIAM STEWART   JOHN SMEATON
LORD PROVOST   ENGINEER
BRIDGE WIDENED 1869
JOHN PULLAR. LORD PROVOST
A. D. STEWART. ENGINEER

Perth Bridge with angler ▷

The angler is dwarfed by the bridge towering over him. His figure gives scale to the stout strength of its proportions.

Perth Bridge and Potterhill Flats ▷

The contrast of old and new is nowadays evident in most cities. Sometimes it is thrust upon us. When the flats were built in 1960 opinions differed about their stark obtrusiveness on the city scene, but this is thankfully now softened by the passage of time and the growth of the trees.

The Old Academy, Rose Terrace

This building stands as the centrepiece of Rose Terrace (q.v.) giving an added grandeur to an already distinguished row. The foundation stone was laid on 19th October 1803 and the building officially opened as a school in September 1807. The architect was Robert Reid. It was designed to bring under one roof the following: Perth Academy, Perth Grammar School, The English School, The French School, Drawing and Painting School, and Writing School. Later (1915) Sharp's Institution was incorporated. The Academy was built by public subscription at a cost of £7,000, the site having been given by Thomas Hay Marshall.

Architectural Note: The building is described as being of two storeys and basement with symmetrical ashlar five-window front and having a rusticated ground floor. The centre three bays are recessed with arched tripartites at ground floor and coupled Roman Doric arch at first-floor level. There is a balustraded parapet with clock and statue of Britannia added (sculptor, John Rhind, 1884). The interior is plain with notable octagonal room at rear. This room with its decorated plaster ceiling and tall windows is one of the finest examples of Georgian workmanship outside Edinburgh. Listed "A" in an "A" group.

The Old Academy, from the north

Seen to advantage in morning sunlight. As it faces the east, the facade is deserted by the sun before midday.

The Old Academy

The upright format seems to impart a lofty dignity to the building, not so evident in the wide frame. This emphasises the importance of viewpoint.

Rose Terrace

Authoritatively described as "the grandest palace-fronted terrace in Scotland, outside Edinburgh".

Handsomely arranged about the imposing centrepiece of the Old Academy (q.v.) it faces eastwards across the broad acres of the North Inch. The River Tay runs parallel a few hundred yards distant and beyond it rise the lands of Kincarrathie, Murrayshall, Deuchney and Kinnoull. The terrace, named after the wife of Provost Hay Marshall — Rose — was designed by the architect Robert Reid and completed in 1805. It is three-storeyed with basement in classic ashlar and with a rusticated ground floor. Listed an "A" group.

Atholl Crescent: Panorama

Panoramic view taken from North Inch on a Spring morning. On left the buildings, in shadow, of Blackfriars Street. In centre, Atholl Crescent, and on right, Rose Terrace.

◁ *Interior of Masonic Lodge: No. 5 Atholl Crescent*

Looking upwards from the entrance hall, the graceful elegance of stair balustrade, plaster ceiling and roof light blend in a tasteful unison.

Atholl Place

All of the buildings, Nos. 1-6, in this Georgian Terrace were commenced by 1797 and completed before 1805 when they appeared in maps of that year. Architecturally they are described as forming a classic terrace of two-storeys with basement and attics. Each house is three windows wide with pilastered fan light doorpieces. No. 6 was later raised slightly. Listed "B": part of an "A" group.

◁ *Atholl Crescent*

The only crescent in the Georgian suburb of the time, this was built about the same time as Rose Terrace and finished in 1805. The work was probably supervised by Robert Reid if not entirely his design. It is classic in design; is two-storeyed with basement, ashlar built and painted. The centre house (now Masonic Lodge) is pedimented with a Roman Doric doorway. See photograph of interior: All Nos. from 2-8 are listed "A" in an "A" group.

Upper Mill

The City Mills

Situated on the King's Lade the mills consist of three blocks, the upper and lower mills and a tall granary block (q.v.). The upper mills shown here are much older than the lower. Two 15 feet internal wheels turned great tree-trunk columns which gave power to machinery made in the mid-19th century. The main roof is of remarkable construction — King post with radial struts at the piended ends. The lower mills are neatly dated between 1805 and 1810 by the maps of these years and have a water wheel of 16 feet in diameter and 14 feet 6 inches wide. The upper mills have been converted with respect to their history, into a hotel and in 1983 the lower mills were restored both externally and internally. Listed "A".

Lower Mill

Granary Building, City Mills

Tall slim building with stair tower, mid-18th century. Was restored in 1984.

Historical Note: The City Mills were originally the King's Mills; traditionally given to Malcolm Canmore by a Mercer. They were subsequently returned to the city fathers by King Robert III. Until now the City Mills is the only urban mill complex to remain anything like complete since the destruction of Edinburgh's Bonnington Mills in 1983. The granary, high and narrow is quite different in proportion from the low and wide Bonnington example.

Lower City Mill with Lade

Before restoration in 1983.

Original Driving Wheel

Photographed at time of conversion of the upper mills into the City Mills Hotel. Note the wooden teeth.

The Old Waterworks

The Old Waterworks, otherwise "The Round House"; Marshall Place

The original building was designed and the water pump planned by Dr Adam Anderson, LL.D., F.R.S.L. and E., Rector of Perth Academy and later Professor of Natural Philosophy at the University of St Andrews. Authority was given under the town's first Water Act which came into force with the Royal Assent in 1829. The building was completed in 1832.

Paying due respect to the neighbouring Georgian Terraces on Marshall Place (q.v.), still comparatively new, Dr Anderson chose a classical style of design in order to add grace and dignity to function. The result was as we see it today, after the removal of later buildings (1973) and restoration of the main body (1974). (A complete photographic record of this renovation work is available in the A. K. Bell Library.)

The basic concept of the original scheme was to raise water from the River Tay, using a steam pump, and store the water in a high tank from which it could be piped to the taps in the town. In detail this meant constructing an intake for water in the river and leading it to filter beds at Moncrieffe Island; then after filtration taking it in a pipe (12 inch cast iron) under the river to wells sunk beneath the waterworks from which the steam engines would pump it to the tank in the upper part of the rotunda. This, then, became the town's reservoir. Pipelines took the water to street wells in the town and some residences which were at a level lower than that of the water standing in the tank. The inscription above the door describes the action in a few Latin words: Aquam igne et aqua haurio —"I draw water by fire and water".

So successful was the result that the King of Prussia asked for a similar works to be built in Berlin — 1837.

In 1965 however the works in Marshall Place were closed down having become obsolete with the introduction of a modern water supply, and the building came under consideration for demolition. Fortunately the body known as the Perth Civic Trust came into being (1967) and was able to convince the local water authority that in terms of the city's heritage they were in possession of a treasure beyond price — a gem of history — something to be cherished with loving care. The tide turned. Restoration was commenced in 1972 and finished in 1974.

It is fitting that this unique building be now, 1996, in use as an art gallery. It is listed "A".

The architects for the restoration were Morris & Steedman, Edinburgh.

Waterworks: restoration under way

The recent engine house has been demolished (May 1973) and restoration work on the original building commenced.

Waterworks, before restoration

This photograph, taken at the time the building and machinery were declared obsolete and considered by some to be fit only for demolition, shows the original building in the background with a more recent addition built to house a more efficient engine, in the foreground.

Before the restoration of the original building could be commenced this recent addition had to be completely cleared away.

Waterworks: further progress in restoration

The top of the old chimney stack has been removed and work commenced on cleaning the stone of the lower part of the rotunda. The upper part of the latter — the cast iron cistern tank — has been repaired, repainted, volutes and friezes replaced where necessary and the blind consoled windows refixed.

Waterworks restoration

A replica of the original urn, made of glass fibre, is ready for hoisting into place on top of the chimney. It is seen here in the builders' yard.

Waterworks restoration

Stonemason preparing stone for replacement.

Waterworks restoration

With a raised finger the steeplejack controls the delicate operation of lowering and positioning the urn — the finishing touch.

King James VI Hospital

The southern aspect.

The hospital was founded under two royal charters, the first, 9th August 1569, during the minority of the King, then aged two years, and the second, 29th July 1587 when the King was 20. They were confirmed by the Scottish parliament. The ministers and elders of the city churches were constituted governors; the churches now concerned being St John's, St Paul's and St Mark's, and their charges "the puir memberis of Jesus Christ, now and in all times cuming dwelling and resident within the Burgh of Perth".

During the early part of the 18th century irregularities in the administration of Hospital funds resulted in an action in the Court of Session. It was not until 1750 that the present building through the efforts of Bailie Robertson and Deacon Gardiner was erected. Sited where the old Carthusian Monastery stood before the Reformation, the foundation stone was laid by Provost Cree.

Whereas originally the hospital provided not only shelter but work for the residents it is now in the nature of sheltered housing for small family units in flats under the immediate supervision of a Hospital Master appointed by the committee of management. The committee room (q.v.) situated in the south-west wing of the building, has great charm of atmosphere but it is the air of history that

The northern aspect.

is most telling. Christian liberty is faithfully recorded on every panel of the room, dating from the 16th century and finishing with the record (q.v.) of the funding of the restoration in 1973-75.

The cupola, complete with clock and bell, was presented by the Duke of Atholl in 1764 following the demolition of the House of Nairne (architect Sir Wm Bruce).

Architectural Notes: The hospital is built on an H plan in the fashion of the late 18th century with scale and platt stair in centre, having central spine wall ending in half columns. It is the largest building of its size and type to remain extant, similar structures in Edinburgh, Glasgow, Dundee and elsewhere having disappeared. Listed "A".

King James VI Hospital

The northern aspect, floodlit in 1976 after the restoration.

King James VI Hospital: Committee Room ▷

The Chairman's eye view of the committee room. Sums of money "doted" for the upkeep of the hospital were carefully inscribed on the walls for all to see. On the right of the photograph the door of the cast iron safe can be seen. The safe was made in Perth Foundry in 1825.

Interior of Committee Room: King James VI Hospital

Looking towards "the chair" there is the atmosphere of Christian benevolence throughout the centuries.

Detail of bell in central cupola: King James VI Hospital

From the House of Nairne after its demolition in 1764, presented by the Duke of Atholl. The inscription reads: "For my Lord Nairne Robertus Maxvell me fecit 1712".

Inscribed Panel in Committee Room: King James VI Hospital

The most recent inscription, the latest of many benefactions.

KING JAMES VI HOSPITAL
RESTORATION: 1973-75

THIS PROGRAMME, INVOLVING MUCH INTERNAL RECONSTRUCTION OF THE BUILDING AS WELL AS MEASURES TO PRESERVE AND ENHANCE ITS EXTERNAL ASPECT, WAS MADE POSSIBLE ONLY WITH THE SPLENDID PROMISE OF AS MUCH AS £100,000 FROM THE GANNOCHY TRUST. FOR THIS THE HOSPITAL MANAGERS RECORD THEIR DEEP AND ABIDING GRATITUDE. THE SCHEME HAD VALUABLE AID ALSO FROM STATE GRANT(£37,800). IN THE RESULT 21 WELL APPOINTED MODERN FLATS WERE PROVIDED FOR LETTING, IN PLACE OF 15 SUB-STANDARD FLATS, A MISSION HALL AND SOME CELLAR SPACE.

THUS THROUGH SUPPORT ON A SCALE FAR BEYOND THEIR OWN RESOURCES THE MANAGERS WERE ENABLED TO REALISE A CHERISHED HOPE FOR THE CONTINUING USEFULNESS OF THEIR HOSPITAL HOUSE, KENSPECKLE SINCE 1750 IN THE COMMUNITY OF PERTH WHICH IT WAS BUILT TO SERVE.

John L. Brown, Convener, Improvements Committee.
James A. Smellie, Hospital Master.
James Morrison, Architect.

The central cupola: King James VI Hospital

Was the gift of the Duke of Atholl in 1764 having been part of the House of Nairne, Strathord, which was designed by Sir Wm. Bruce.

Charlotte Street/Charlotte Place, corner building

Plans for Charlotte Street were laid out as early as 1783 but this building does not appear on maps until 1792. It is an imposing building, apparently conscious of the advantage of its position overlooking the North Inch.

Architectural Note: Neo-Greek in style, four-storeyed, ashlar. Greek Doric columned ground floor on Charlotte Place. Balcony. Has four-window front with three-window bow to Charlotte Place and three-window front to Charlotte Street. Listed "A".

Spires of St Leonard's in the Fields and St John's Kirk as seen from South Inch

A comparative view. The crown spire of the former and the lead covered octagonal broach spire of St John's.

◁ ## St Leonard's in the Fields Church

One of the most notable buildings in Perth. Its crown tower dominates the skyline of the city when viewed from the South Inch. It was designed by J. J. Stevenson in 1885 being an example of late Scots Gothic revival of exceptional merit. Its heavy buttresses are one of its outstanding external features while the aisled nave with clear-storey are two of the internal. The local architects were Smart, Stewart and Mitchell. It is an "A" listed building.

The buildings of Marshall Place are seen on the right and those of King's Place and King James Place on the left.

◁ ## Marshall Place with St Leonard's in the Fields Church (centre) and statue of Sir Walter Scott (left)

View taken from the entrance to South Inch opposite King Street.

Old Toll House, Barnhill

Is situated on the Dundee road at the boundary between the estates of Barnhill and Kinfauns. Erected in early 19th century when the toll road was opened — 1829. The architect was probably Wm. Mackenzie. It is an uncommonly sophisticated toll house, built in ashlar and having one-storey only but with basement in fall of the ground. The centre bay projects with Greek Doric columns and the roof is piended. Listed "A". Bill of Tolls at right (q.v.).

Barnhill Bar ▷

If this notice be read "Barnhill Barrier" the meaning becomes clear. (It has no connection with the supply of liquid refreshment.) The bar or barrier consisted of a stout length of wood stretched across the roadway barring the way to travellers until their dues were paid. On the opposite side of the road from the toll house the socket into which the bar fitted is still to be seen in the stonework. The bill of charges is self explanatory.

BARNHILL BAR

BY ORDER *of the* TRUSTEES
TOLLS PAYABLE HERE.

		£ S D
For every Coach, Barouche & Drawn by 1 Horse		,, 1 ,,
Dº	by 2 Dº	,, 2 ,,
Dº	by 3 Dº	,, 3 ,,
Dº	by 4 Dº	,, 4 ,,
Dº	by 5 Dº	,, 5 ,,
Dº	by 6 Dº	,, 6 ,,
For every Waggon, Cart & Drawn by 1 Horse		
Ox or Beast of Draught.		,, 1 ,,
Dº	by 2 Dº	,, 1 6
Dº	by 3 Dº	,, 2 ,,
Dº	by 4 Dº	,, 3 ,,
Dº	by 5 Dº	,, 3 6
Dº	by 6 Dº	,, 5 ,,
Dº	by 7 Dº	,, 6 ,,
Dº	by 8 Dº	,, 8 ,,
For each Horse, Mule or Ass, Laden or Unladen		,, ,, 4
For every score of Neat Cattle -----		,, 1 ,,
And so in proportion for any greater or Lesser number not under Eleven ----		
For every half Score of Oxen or Neat Cattle		,, ,, 8
For each Ox &c when the number is Less than 10		,, ,, 1
For every score of Calves, Hogs, Goats or Lambs		,, ,, 6
For every half Score of Calves &c -----		,, ,, 4
For every Calf, Hog &c when number Less than 10		,, ,, ½

Horses Travelling for hire under the Post-Horse
Duty Acts drawing any Carriage for which Toll
Has been paid, to be made free on returning
Either without such Carriage or with same,
It being empty & without a ticket denoting
A fresh hiring, provided they return the
Same day or before Nine of the Clock of the
Morning the succeeding day. Horses travelling
So, passing through a Toll-bar without a
Carriage & paying the Toll & returning that
Same day, or before Nine of the Morning of
The succeeding day, the Toll paid previously
For the Horses shall be deducted from that
Of the Carriage.

jas. Mc Tavids
TOLL-KEEPER.

Pitheavlis Castle: 50 Needless Road

The lands of Pitheavlis are recorded as having been sold to a Robert Stewart before 1586. It is possible that he built the castle. By 1636 Patrick, son of Laurence Oliphant of Bachilton :"was served heir in the lands and quarry of Pitheavlis". From the Oliphants it passed to the Murrays of Elibank following a link by marriage in 1803. The last of the family to hold the property was M. F. Oliphant-Murray, Viscount Elibank, until 1920 when it became the property of Sir Robert Usher, Bart. It then passed to John Fraser, auctioneer, and finally, and until the present time, to the Perth District Council.

Architectural Note: Late 16th century castle with three-storeys and attic in L-plan. Harled greywashed, crowstepped gables. Circular rear turret stair. South-west jamb has twin pepperpot turrets. Listed "A".

St John's Street: Bank of Scotland and adjoining buildings

The bank building (left) is of outstanding architectural interest and is listed "A". The architect was David Rhind. Italian Renaissance in style it was built in 1846. Other of its features are its Roman Doric pilastered end doorpieces and balustraded area ground floor also its pedimented windows and balustraded balcony at first floor. The photograph was taken in 1970 and also shows adjoining buildings — Nos. 56-70. Those include McEwen's of Perth (centre) built in 1846-47 and designed by the same architect — David Rhind. It is a single-storey block, originally of three shops with consoled cornice and balustraded parapet. Listed "B" in an "A" group. Further to right, Nos. 58-70. The building having seven windows on first and second floors and a wallhead gable, of period 1796-1801, is listed "B" in the "A" group. Finally the corner building viz. Nos. 72-76, of late 1790's is listed "B" in the same "A" group. An inscription (q.v.) referring to Gavin Douglas, Bishop of Dunkeld, appears in the central, blind, window of this last group.

Ref, "Fountain Close".

Facade of Tay Street looking south from west end of Queen's Bridge

The imposing building which occupies the right half of the photograph is known locally as the "County Buildings". It houses the sheriff court, offices and the county ballroom. Built in 1819 on the site of the original Gowrie House it was designed by Sir Robert Smirke in the neo-Greek style. The frontage bears a striking resemblance to that of the British Museum, London, another of Smirke's works. It is a listed "A". The left half of the photograph contains the Baptist Church, with spire, business premises, Old People's Welfare Hall and club rooms — (formerly the museum of the Perthshire Society of National Science). Finally in the distance, the dome and chimney of the old waterworks are seen on the left (q.v.). The Baptist Church was burned down in 1984.

York Place — The old Infirmary

The foundation stone of the City and County Infirmary was laid in August 1836 by Lord Kinnaird.

Peacock in *Perth, its annals and its archives* wrote that the design is "admirable, forming a prominent public ornament, and a monument to the artistic skill and good taste of Mr W. M. McKenzie, city architect". It provided a much-needed service — "no public receptacle for the diseased, nor for the treatment of sudden or violent injuries having previously existed in the county".

1834 — £400 left by Dr Patrick Brown; £600 left by Marquis of Breadalbane.
By January 1838 — £6,812 had been raised by subscription.
Opened for patients 1st October 1838 — accommodated 84 patients.
Strategically situated where the Glasgow turnpike entered the town.

Architectural Note: Handsome late classical with porte cochère on elevated site. The round arched detail suggests that McKenzie had studied Thomas Hamilton's Dean Orphanage in Edinburgh (1833). The interior was necessarily plain, but the entrance hall has a very fine plaster ceiling in the manner of Sir John Soane.

Historical Note: Following the building of the present Perth Royal Infirmary which in 1913 rendered the old infirmary redundant, the building became the administrative offices of the County Council of Perth and Kinross, and has remained continually in the use of the local authority until today. Conversion from offices to the A.K. Bell Library, which is still under the administration of the local authority, took place from 1991-94. Prince Charles performed the official opening on 13th January, 1995. A.K. Bell was the benefactor who originated and financed the Gannochy Trust whose generous contribution facilitated the conversion of the Old Infirmary to the modern library. The A.K. Bell Library can justly claim to be in the forefront in supplying all forms of library services in this present age.

The Agnus Dei symbol

Long associated with John the Baptist. This circular wood carving of the Agnus Dei, appropriately coloured, looks downwards from the central oilette — a circular opening above the crossing through which the bells were hoisted to the tower. The symbol was an important constituent part, being centrally situated, in the coat of arms of the City of Perth until the latter became incorporated in the District of Perth and Kinross.

St John's Kirk from St Anne's Lane

This section ends as it began with pictures of our greatest heritage — The Kirk of St John the Baptist. The Kirk gave its name to the town — St John's Toun — a name that survived for centuries. But now like many other religious institutions falling membership in the congregation is having its effect, not only on its spiritual influence in the local community but on the financial resources necessary for the upkeep of an old building. It is of course a national monument of the highest importance and as such attracts support grants from various bodies but the local citizens along with the congregation are first in line to contribute to the upkeep of their own town's Kirk, now needing extensive repair. They received the Kirk in good order, after its great restoration, in 1927 as a priceless heritage from their forebears. It is now their noble privilege to take part in passing it on equally resplendent to a new generation educated and sensitive, and entirely fitted to receive it in sacred trust.

II. THE GEORGIAN PERIOD

FOLLOWING in the steps of Edinburgh, Glasgow and Aberdeen the City of Perth was not far behind in acquiring its own Georgian Terraces. Provost Thomas Hay Marshall was the instigator of improvements to the city from 1795 onwards. Being a friend of Robert Reid, later to become the king's architect, he commissioned the latter to build handsome terraces, in the Georgian mould, on both the south and the north sides of the old town, encasing it in a new splendour. Marshall Place fronting on the South Inch appeared in 1801 and Rose Terrace facing the North Inch in 1805. Other architects appeared at the same period bringing their own variants of the Georgian theme, as seen in Atholl Crescent, Atholl Place, Blackfriars House, Charlotte Street and Place, Barossa Place, King's Place and St Leonard's Bank. Examples are set out on the following pages. Those which are listed "A" appeared in Section I.

Statue of Thomas Hay Marshall

Sculptured by a stone mason named Cochrane this life-size statue looks down from the colonnade fronting the rotunda of the art galleries. This rotunda was erected by the citizens of Perth in grateful memory of this provost who did so much to instigate and encourage the advancement of the city in the late 18th and early 19th centuries.

Provost Marshall's House, Rose Terrace

Built as a town house for Thomas Hay Marshall, Provost of Perth 1800-01 and 1804-05. Rose Terrace was named after his wife, Rose. The architect was Robert Reid (1776-1856). Completed in 1805.

Architectural Note: Early 19th century classic, three storey and basement, painted ashlar, four window fronts to Rose Terrace and Atholl Street. Chanelled ground floor, giant order of fluted doric pilasters above, with wrought iron balcony at 1st floor: blocking course at parapet, slated roof.

The classic dignity of this residence amply reflected the importance of its owner. Listed "B" in an "A" group.

Nos. 28/30 High Street   ▷

The "Prudential" office building was the town house of the Mercers of Aldie in the 18th century. This in turn had replaced a hostelry known as "Kitty Reid's House o' the Green" used by golfers of the time. The Arms of Aldie can still be seen on the building. In the 19th century it was the premises of David Morison, printer and publisher, who was the designer of the Marshall Memorial Rotunda.

Architectural Note: The style is provincial Renaissance. The High Street front was re-faced in the mid-19th century. It has a four-storeyed stuccoed front to High Street, superimposed pilasters, architraved windows with segmental pediments at first storey and triangular pediments at second; main cornice. The stucco front of the superimposed pilasters was a mid-19th century embellishment. Formerly the shop front had robust Corinthian capitals carved in timber but it was not found practicable to reuse them. More of its original 18th century character survives in Watergate where there remains a good Gibbsian doorpiece and pilastered shop front (seen in adjoining photograph). Listed "B". Part of an "A" group.

Salutation Hotel, South Street

Inscribed on a large brass plate fixed near the entrance to the hotel are these words: "The Oldest Established Hotel in Scotland (1699)" Extract from an article "Bridging the Time, 1745-1910", from Chambers' Journal of May 1st 1911:—

"Trial of Colonel Bower of Kingaldrum, Forfarshire at York. The only charge that could be brought against him was that he had worn a white cockade in his bonnet and had been seen shaking hands with Prince Charles Edward at the Salutation Inn in Perth".

"The room that Prince Charles Edward occupied is still in use — No. 20." No part of the building of 1699 exists in its present form.

Architectural Note: Eastern part built c. 1800. Impressive by its large Ionic Venetian window at 1st floor handsomely detailed in the manner of Robert Reid and flanked by niches with painted figures of highlanders. Western part, 18th century, partly remodelled mid-19th. Architraved windows and pilastered doorpiece. Listed "B".

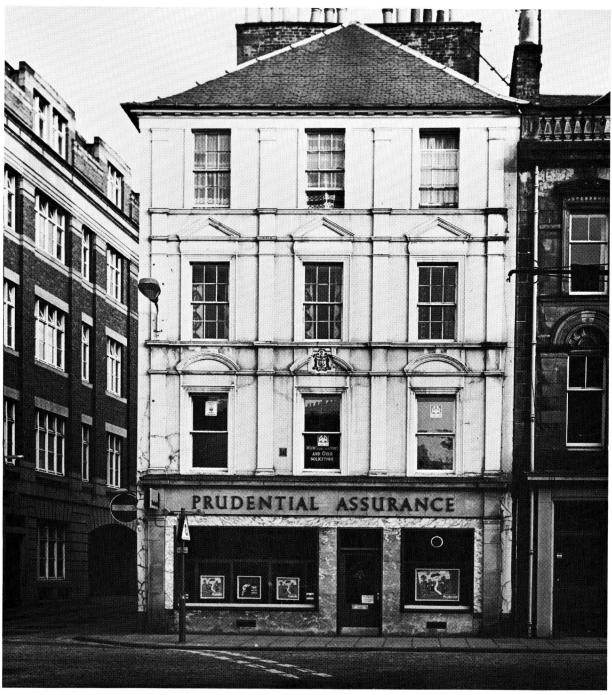

Nos. 3 and 5 Watergate

This attractive side entrance to no. 30 High Street has a Gibbsian doorway of c. 1770. It is adjoined by an old pilastered shop front.

No. 13 High Street

The Cunningham-Graham Close, situated a few yards from the District Council Administrative Offices, is also known as the King's Arms Close. It dates from 1699. The Kings' Arms Inn which was situated to the rear of the close was demolished in 1892. The property above the close was built for Town Clerk Robert Graham at the time of his marriage to Elspeth Cunningham. Their initials appear on the pediment which was a very up to date detail for a provincial town house in 1699. The house is now the oldest inhabited in Perth.

Charlotte Street, west side   (See top of next page.)

Although laid out as early as 1783 Charlotte Street, west side, was probably not built until some years later. It is shown in maps of 1792.

No. 2 is part of the old Post Office building — No. 80 George Street (q.v.).

Nos. 4-8; a three-storey building with five-window frontage, ground floor shops (e.g. "Eagle Star") and central pedimented doorpiece. It has two canted dormers. Listed "B" in an "A" group.

Nos. 10-14 also late 18th century having one additional floor, making four in all. The ground floor (with shops) and first floor are rusticated, the upper floors stuccoed. Listed "B" in an "A" group.

On the extreme left of photograph — no. 77 George Street, a branch of the Bank of Scotland — is listed "B" in a "B" group. Photo: August 1980.

George Street from Perth Bridge (September 1980)

Nos. 75 and 77 George Street on extreme left — Bank of Scotland at corner with Tay Street — was built about 1810; ashlar, having double doorpiece with Ionic columns. Door now altered to windows. Pedimented on Tay Street frontages. Listed "B".

On extreme right: Perth Museum and Art Gallery (q.v.).

In centre: Nos. 62 and 64 George Street and No. 2 Bridge Lane. Late 18th century four-storey building with blind splayed corner. Modern shop below (Hope). Listed "C".

Tay Street/George Street corner

No. 2 Tay Street was said to have been built of the sandstone removed from the parapets of Smeaton's Bridge after it was widened in 1869. Its architecture is described as Thomsonesque Greek of around 1875, in stugged red ashlar — three-storey and basement with three-bay elevation. The outer bays are pedimented. The centre bay is recessed above the doorpiece where there is only one window. Listed "C".

No. 77 George Street (Bank of Scotland) was built around 1810. It has three-storeys and basement in ashlar. There is a six-window front to George Street where there is a double doorpiece with Ionic columns — now altered to windows. It is pedimented on the Tay Street frontage. Listed "B".

On the right the Colonnade and rotunda of the Marshall Monument can be seen and also the pedimented frontage of the old Post Office (q.v.).

▽

Charlotte Street, east side

Charlotte Street was one of the first streets to be laid out 1783 in Perth's Georgian period. It appears on a map of 1792. This is not surprising in view of its proximity to the city, its convenience to the "new" bridge and its position of high amenity adjacent to both the river Tay and the North Inch.

The houses as seen are odd numbered from the right.

Architectural Notes: No. 1 Late 18th century two-storey and basement, three-window painted ashlar building with Corinthian columned doorpiece. Elegant frieze with swags over windows, end pilasters and angle urns, slated roof. Listed "B". Note the fire insurance medallion over main entrance. No. 3 Late 18th century. Similar to above but with attic and Ionic columned doorpiece which is on left front. Window architraved at first floor. Listed "B".

No. 5 Late 18th century, altered mid-19th century, three-window ashlar. Centre pedimented consoled doorpiece, architraved windows with segmental pediments on ground and first floors. Two pilastered and pedimented dormers. Listed "B".

No. 7 (containing "B. & S. Guild") Late 18th century three-storeyed with attic and basement. Piended dormers. Listed "B".

No. 9 Part only seen; three-storey and basement, five-window, attic, chimney gable with Venetian window. Ground floor shop. Listed "B". All Nos. together form part of a group listed "A".

No. 6 Charlotte Street

Locally known as "Eagle Star Close" from the premises adjoining, No. 6 Charlotte Street contains this beautiful geometrical stair. Arresting in its effect when viewed from above, the design is enhanced by the well wrought wooden handrail. Craftsmen of the time who have left us this heritage deserve great credit for their enduring skill. The building is Listed "B", and is part of an "A" group.

Panorama from North Inch

All the buildings in this panoramic view from the North Inch were built at the turn of 18th-19th centuries. They constitute the main part of what is known as the Northern Georgian Town. Left to right: Charlotte Street, Charlotte Place, Albert Monument, Blackfriars House, Atholl Place, Blackfriars Street, Atholl Crescent.

Atholl Crescent (left) and Rose Terrace (right)

Parts of each row blend together architecturally as viewed from the edge of the North Inch. Provost Marshall's House (q.v.) is predominant reflecting the owner's importance.

Marshall Place, Nos. 15-28 ▷

Seen on the right, this terrace block is the second of two blocks designed by Robert Reid in association with Provost Hay Marshall. The first is in line, but nearer to the river Tay and is serially numbered 1-14. Reid was aged 26 in the year 1800 when the project began and eight years later was to become the king's Master of Works and Architect in Scotland. It was the original intention to build a third block in line but with changing circumstances St Leonards in the Fields Church was erected on the site. King's Place and King James Place were built later continuing the line beyond the church (q.v.). The result has been an interesting facade to the south and to those travelling from that direction on the Edinburgh Road, even an arresting one.

Architectural Note: Begun in 1801 this block is an astylar terrace of two-storeys with attics and basement. The centre and end sections are three-storeyed, advanced, with main door entrances and lunettes at third-storey. The building is in ashlar, part painted. Listed "B".

Statue of Sir Walter Scott ▷

Situated in Marshall Place, south side, facing towards King Street, this statue shows Sir Walter pedestrian with his dog. It is on record as having been "accidentally acquired by the magistrates at the sale of a local sculptor's stock", the sculptor, a stone mason named Cochrane, having emigrated to Australia. Mid-19th century.

Barossa Place: Nos. 3, 5, 7 and 9

Named after the battle in the Peninsular War commemorating victory of Thomas Graham of Balgowan, General Lord Lynedoch, Barossa Place forms part of the northern suburb of Perth which was built in the early 19th century. A classic terrace, painted ashlar. Nos. 3 and 5 — rusticated ground floor. No. 7 pilastered ground floor. All listed "B" in an "A" group.

Barossa Place/Melville Street junction

In the foreground is Melville Street and on the left the two houses seen are in Barossa Place —
Nos. 29 and 31. The latter, otherwise known as Lynedoch House was named after Thomas Graham
of Balgowan, General Lord Lynedoch one of Wellington's generals in the Peninsular War. Built
about 1830 it has a Greek Doric columned porch, main cornice, blocking course and long modern
dormer; also a single storey extension to west. Listed "B".

On the right of the picture is the villa, Santa Monica, 25 Melville Street, cornering on Barossa
Place. Built in the mid-19th century it has two storeys, ashlar masonry with channelled ground floor
and pilastered doorpiece. Three architraved windows at first floor. Listed "B".

In the foreground is Melville Street — named after Henry Dundas, 1st Viscount Melville, Baron
Dunira in the County of Perth (1742-1811), the eminent politician known as the Master of Scotland.

III. PUBLIC BUILDINGS, CHURCHES

IN this section we have included a selection of notable buildings — Victorian mostly — which reflect the taste of the civic authorities and kirk sessions of the time. Also included are the graveyards of Greyfriars and Kinnoull, and two school buildings. Several are listed "B" or "C" but it is to be noted that all "A" listed buildings are concentrated in Section 1.

Victorian Dignity

From a viewpoint on Perth Bridge the detail of the buildings is brought out with the use of a long focus lens on the camera. The spire of St Matthew's Church soars above both the General Accident building (centre) and the District Council building (right). The latter two buildings were both to come under Local Authority administration in 1983. Each building on the photograph forms part of a listed "A" group.

District Council Chambers: High Street/Tay Street corner

This building occupies the traditional site used for civic buildings in Perth since mediaeval times. The main approach to the town for travellers and goods was by river-boat or ferry to the merchants' quay which was situated at this spot. The tolbooth, guard room, court room, council chamber, tron and pillory were all within a few paces distant, and the cross of Perth a mere 50 yards away. The town crier would make his proclamations "by tuck of drum" for all to hear within its precincts and these would include ships tied up at the quay.

The distinctive turret at the corner of the building has its own history. Tradition has it that when most of the town was inundated and destroyed by a flood in 1210, subsequent rebuilding included part of the adjacent Chapel of our Lady. Whether the first turret took shape at that time is impossible to say. A painting of early 18th century period shows a tall pointed turret which must have dominated the skyline on the riverside. The architect of this is unknown but Andrew Heiton the architect of the present building in 1879 gave due respect to history in his design, incorporating the handsome turret seen. Listed "B".

High Points, Tay Street

The spires of the District Council Offices (right) and St Matthew's Church (left) stand high with the cupola of the former General Accident Assurance building between them. The three buildings are each listed "B", in an "A" group.

District Council Chambers: Front to High Street with Entrance
Note the Provosts' Lamps

In 1984 the District Administration moved to No. 2 High Street — the previous premises of the General Accident Fire Life Assurance Corporation, they having moved their head office to their new building at Pitheavlis.

The above building was retained by the local authority for the Leisure and Recreation Department.

Civic Symbols

This photograph has a prophetic side. The civic lamp and the building in the background are separated by the width of the High Street and at the time of the photograph in May 1981 were quite unconnected. But since then the hand of history has been at work. The building has become "civic" too, having been taken over by the District Council for use as their headquarters in 1984.

The General Accident Building in Festival Finery ▷

The General Accident Fire and Life Assurance Corporation Limited was formed as a direct consequence of the Employers Liability Act (1880) which made it compulsory for employers to compensate their workers for any injuries sustained while at work.

The General Accident was set up in 1885 to provide local farmers and others with the insurance they needed under the new act.

An office was opened at 44 Tay Street and four clerks were employed.

In 1887 Francis Norie-Miller was appointed as manager at the age of 27. His energy and business

acumen turned the firm from a small local concern into the International Company that it is today. This building has served the company as headquarters from 1895 to 1983.

A single new headquarters at Pitheavlis was opened replacing the High Street building and others throughout the city. The South Street/St John's Place branch office remains open for local customers and the archive and museum continue to be housed in the original building at 44 Tay Street.

Architectural note: Designed by George P.K. Young 1895: really by Cedric Young who had been with J.J. (Sir John) Burnet in Glasgow, and whose Glasgow commercial buildings the General Accident strongly reflects with its baroque detail colonnaded eaves gallery. J.J. Burnet was subsequently to design the General Accident's London building. Additions to Perth building are in similar but plainer style; 1953-54. Messrs. G.P.K. Young.

F

The former General Accident Building

Facade to Tay Street

The General Accident Building: Floodlit, 1960
As seen from Bridgend on the occasion of the 75th anniversary of the founding of the Corporation.

The Spire, St Matthew's Church, Tay Street ▷

Probably Perth's most prominent landmark.

It was during the ministry of Reverend John Laidlaw that the West Church — now St Matthew's — was built on Tay Street.

At the end of 1863 Mr Turnbull of Huntingtowerfield purchased the necessary properties between the Tay and the Watergate for £2,300. This greatly facilitated the opening up of Tay Street.

Mr Turnbull's original proposal was for three churches under one roof thus rehousing Free St Leonard's, Free Middle and Free West, however the former two pulled out of the venture.

On 4th November 1868 it was resolved to erect a new Free West Church — and a sum of £6,000 was agreed. (Old West Church was in Mill Street on site of Dept. of Health and Social Security.)

The author of the pamphlet published in 1951 writes "its style was that of the early English Gothic of about the middle of the 13th Century but as plainly treated as possible".

Height from pavement to top of steeple — 212 feet.

18.5.1870 Memorial stone laid by the Earl of Dalhousie.

23.11.1871 Opened for public worship.

In 1965, four congregations were merged in St Matthew's — the Wilson Church, Scott Street, the West and Middle Churches in Tay Street and Bridgend Church.

When the church hall and domestic offices were rebuilt, stones from each of the four churches were incorporated.

Architectural Note: Designed by John Honeyman of Glasgow (1831-1914) a distinguished scholar architect who originally trained for the Ministry and received many Church commissions from former fellow students. His most ambitious churches were Glasgow Lansdowne (1861-63) and St Michael's, Slateford, Edinburgh (1883) the spire of which was not built though the tower was completed to the belfry stage. St Matthew's is a less ambitious church, but the spire with its open belfry stage is perhaps the best he built, less tall than the Lansdowne one but happier in proportion. Listed "B" in an "A" group.

Facade: Tay Street

As viewed from the south, four important buildings are seen here as a group. Left to right: St Matthew's Church, Savings Bank, General Accident Building (now vacated), and the tower and spire of the District Council offices (formerly, the City Chambers). Three of these buildings, viz, St Matthews Church, the General Accident building and the District Council Chambers are dealt with under separate photographs (q.v.). The fourth, the Savings Bank, is described as follows:

The architect of the former Savings Bank building (centre) was the city architect — Andrew Heiton. It was erected 1873-75 and officially opened to the public 27th September 1876. The bank formerly occupied premises at 24 Charlotte Street.

Architectural Note: Mid-Victorian Renaissance style: two French roofed pavilions and recessed centre bay in local sandstone with white sandstone dressings. Arched doorpiece south pavilion, matching wooden doorpiece to north. Triple arched centre window. Balustraded parapet with finials. Listed "B".

Balhousie Castle

The original castle of which the remains are incorporated in the present building, first belonged to the Eviot family, 1422. Then it passed to Robert Mercer, 1478 and subsequently to the Hays, Earls of Kinnoull. Reconstruction for the 11th Earl was carried out in 1864 by David Smart, a Perth architect who applied the ideas of David Bryce, Edinburgh, for whom he formerly worked. Bryce was a specialist in the design of great baronial country houses of which Balhousie Castle is an example. Built on L plan, Listed "B". Now in use as the administration H.Q. of the Black Watch Regiment and as their Regimental Museum.

City Hall, King Edward Street

An impressive Edwardian building, the result of a major open competition assessed by Sir John Burnet of Glasgow and London. Architect: Henry Edward Clifford of Glasgow (died 1932). Primarily a church architect he had notable success also in his domestic work but for the city hall he adopted a full Edwardian neo-baroque manner. Opened on 29th April 1911, the hall accommodated 2,100. The small hall accommodated 500. The cost: £30,000. Listed "B".

Nos. 22-26 King Edward Street (right)

Early occupiers of this building were Stewart & Dick, provision merchants; later it was a labour exchange and then Peter Thomson, whiskey blender and wine importer. It is described as a simple Victorian Renaissance building in a corner situation with frontages to King Edward Street and South St John's Place. The corner rises to a fish-scale truncated pyramidal roof with wrought iron cresting.

Kinnoull Parish Church

This church replaced the old parish church of which only a part remains — Kinnoull Aisle (q.v.) — situated in the old churchyard to the south of Queen's Bridge.

The architect was Wm. Burn of Edinburgh who had done other commissions in the area, being favoured by many county families of the time. The building contractor was Wm. Hogg, Forfar. It was officially opened on 15th April 1827 by Reverend W. A. Thomson, minister of the Middle Church. The cost: £3,873 15s. 6d.

Architectural Note: Built in neo-perpendicular style, ashlar, with spired octagonal belfry and porch at east gable: Pinnacled buttresses. The clock is dated 1885. John Ruskin's comment: "Not a high kind of architecture but perfect of its kind". Listed "B".

Kinnoull Parish Church: Interior

This shows the result of internal rearrangements made in 1930 and 1977 (which was the 150th Anniversary of the completion of the present building). In 1930 there was the removal of Galleries and stone staircases: overhaul of the pipe organ: reseating of the area: new pulpit, font, and communion table.

In 1977 there was resiting of the organ and refurbishment of the choir furnishings.

Of greater note is the painted west window — the work of Sir John E Millais, R.A., representing 14 of the parables of our lord. The work was commissioned by and presented to the church by George Gray of Bowerswell, father-in-law of the artist. The original drawings on which the paintings were based were commissioned by the Dalziel Brothers, wood engravers, from Millais in 1857. The artist, who took six years to his task wrote: "I exert myself to the utmost to make them as complete as possible".

Kinnoull Church from Tay Street

This view shows the church (q.v.) from the west bank of the river Tay. The west window, otherwise known as the Millais Window is clearly seen between the riverside trees. Its subject matter is best seen from the interior of the church (q.v.).

Kinnoull Aisle: Old Kinnoull Churchyard

The aisle, or transept, is all that remains of the old Kinnoull Church; probably 16th century. It is a rubble rectangle protected from the weather by a corrugated asbestos roof. It contains a mural monument (q.v.) to George Hay, first Lord Chancellor of Scotland (d. 1634). The church had been rebuilt and enlarged in 1779 but was finally vacated in 1827 when the present church was dedicated. Listed "B".

Tomb of George Hay, First Earl of Kinnoull, D. 1634

Situated in Kinnoull Aisle (q.v.) this elaborate monument was created c. 1635. Two and a half centuries later, 1890, it was restored by the 12th Earl. Now, in 1995, it is in need of further preservation. George Hay was Lord Chancellor of Scotland to King Charles I. Picture—a montage from 3 negatives, 1970.

Note: The town house of George Hay — Hay's Lodging — situated in Watergate near South Street came under a demolition order in 1966 and was demolished in 1967.

Kinnoull Churchyard: Stone to Robert Knox, Boatman

One of several interesting old stones. Inscription is decipherable.

Reverse of gravestone bears a sculptured picture of the ferryman crossing the Tay in his boat. The stone is red sandstone.

Kinnoull Churchyard is situated round the site of the old church of Kinnoull. All that remains today is the ruined foundation and the Kinnoull aisle (q.v.) which was a transept of the old church which was built about 1779.

Greyfriars Burial Ground, Canal Street

A plaque at the entrance states: "The monastery of the Franciscan or Grey Friars, founded in 1460 stood within these grounds which were converted into a burial ground in 1580". The graveyard succeeded the Kirkyard of St John's for interments and when burials within the kirk became no longer permitted. Many interesting headstones marking the graves of guildsmen and craftsmen are to be found here. A notable example is that of John Mylne (q.v.), Master Mason. The graveyard is preserved as a listed building grade "B". It was the only burial ground in Perth until 1849 when Wellshill cemetery was opened.

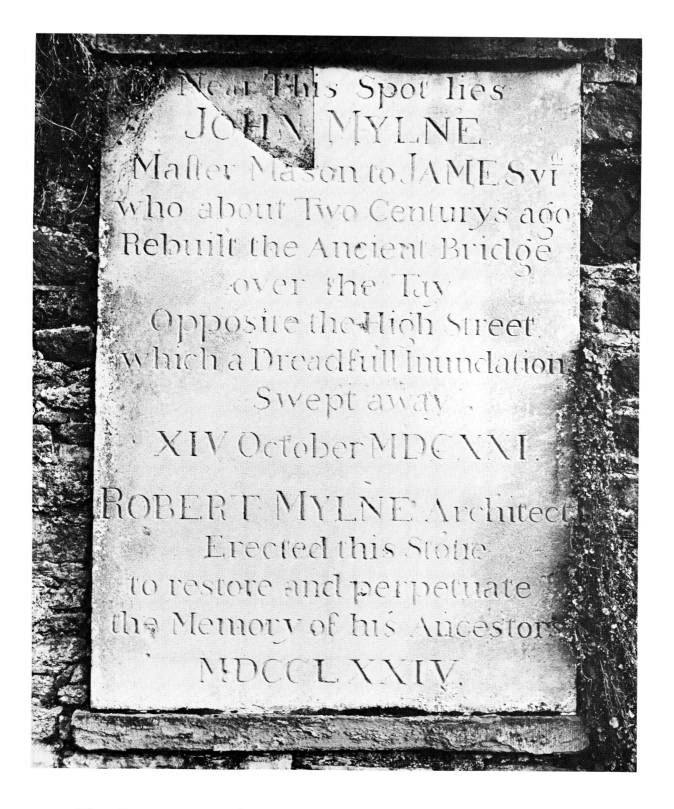

The Gravestone of John Mylne: Greyfriars Burial Ground

The inscription is as follows: "Near This spot lies John Mylne, Master Mason to James VI who about Two centuries ago Rebuilt the Ancient Bridge over the Tay Opposite the High Street which a Dreadfull Inundation Swept away XIV October MDCXXI. Robert Mylne, Architect Erected this Stone to restore and perpetuate the Memory of his Ancestor. MDCCLXXIV".

St Ninian's Cathedral, Scottish Episcopal, Atholl Street

In the wake of the Oxford Movement the Reverend J. C. Chambers was entrusted with the task of opening a mission in Perth. His first service was held in a hall in Atholl Street on 30th November 1846.

Daily prayers, frequent communions and choral services were introduced.

The determination of the Puseyite movement to extend from Oxford to all parts of the country meant that Perth was seen as a natural centre for Scotland.

By 1849 the Bishop wrote to Chambers that "Nothing is wanting to your mission but the erection of a church, which I trust will be commenced early in the spring". — however it was not a church but "a great cathedral" that was to be built.

Six thousand pounds was raised and the foundation stone laid by Bishop Forbes on St Ninian's Day 1849. The cathedral was completed by December 1850.

Architectural Note: St Ninian's Cathedral is a remarkable chronicle of changing fashion in Anglican church design. Building of the cathedral was promoted by the Earl of Glasgow who stipulated that he preferred architect, William Butterfield (1814-1900) of London, be engaged to design it. Glasgow also employed Butterfield to design the Cathedral of the Isles and the associated college at Millport, Cumbrae in the same year. Butterfield was an enthusiast for polychromy, but at Perth his enthusiasm for colour shows only in the original reredos now divided between the vestries. Only the choir, transepts and one bay of the nave were built in 1849-50. Glasgow became over extended on yachting and supporting the Episcopal church and had eventually to withdraw his support. In 1888-90, however, the remainder of the nave was built to Butterfield's design together with the stump of the intended western tower. This work caused problems, and in the later 1890's an architect more in touch with the taste of the times, John Loughborough Pearson (1817-97) was called in. He died while work was still at sketch plan stage, but between 1901 and 1911 his son Frank carried out his intentions, eliminating the western tower by extending the roof over it, and adding the pinnacles of the western gable, which were matched up at the east end, also reconstructed with flanking south aisle and lady chapel. The chancel was also refurnished with new choir stalls, bishop's throne, pulpit and high altar, all to Pearson's design. Finally in 1924 Sir Ninian Comper (1864-1960) replaced the rood screen, Butterfield's being re-used at St Devenick's Bieldside.

Pearson also added the south cloister, vestries and chapter house, extended by a new cloister and recreation hall by Tarbolton and Ochterlony in 1939.

The North Church and Sandeman Library

The North Church (right) began its separate existence in 1747, the original building being replaced in 1792 at a cost of £1,112. The present building with seating for 1,200 and costing £7,000 was opened in 1880. The architect was T.L. Watson of Glasgow, his style being Romanesque of Italian inspiration. It is built in ashlar on a rectangular plan, is unaisled with gable front and open porch. The interior has cast iron columns with galleries.

The Sandeman Library (left) was the gift of Archibald Sandeman who left the residue of his estate — over £30,000 — for the funding of a free library in Perth. He had been a fellow and a tutor at Queen's College, Cambridge and later Professor of Mathematics and Natural Philosophy at Queen's College, Manchester. The building was designed by Messrs Campbell, Douglas and Morrison of Glasgow who were successful in open competition. It is a very handsome example of the free Renaissance in vogue in the late 1890s. It was completed in 1898 and opened by the Earl of Roseberry on 22nd October 1898. Listed "C".

The Library closed in October 1994 when library services were transferred to the new A.K. Bell Library in York Place.

G

St Leonard's Church, King Street

Built by subscription in 1834 at a cost of £2,450.

Architectural Note: Elegant neo-classical design, probably of French inspiration by Wm. MacDonald Mackenzie, City Architect (d. 1856). Described by Peacock as a very handsome chapel "with elegant erection over the portico in miniature imitation of the Choragic Monument of Lysikrates . . ." (This latter is also known as the Lantern of Demosthenes and is situated on the slopes of the Acropolis, Athens). The interior was recast with the addition of an apse in 1891. "Chastely elegant" and "considerable taste" were phrases used in describing its appeal.

The Middle Kirk, Tay Street

The majority of the congregation of the Middle Parish Church formed the "Free Middle" church congregation in 1843 after the Disruption. Led by Dr W. Aird Thomson they worshipped in the Church school and later in the old Wesleyan Chapel, South Street, until their own church was built in Blackfriar's Street (October 1843). This served for 40 years when moves were made to build a new church which was opened a year later. In 1965 the congregation united with those of Bridgend Church, Wilson Church and the West Church to form St Matthew's in whose building the united congregation now worships. The Church was converted in 1995 to provide a number of residential flats. Listed "B".

Architectural Note: Architect — Hippolyte Jean Blanc, 1886. Early pointed in styles, the church is cruciform, with wide five-bay nave, aisles, clearstorey and flying buttresses. It has a rose window to north and north-east porch and double-windowed transept. There is a two-storeyed, with attic, hall at south. Build in red snecked rubble, elaborately detailed, it has a high slated roof with central fleche. The interior has twin arched transepts with galleries and the arcades have circular piers and diapered spandrels.

Kinnoull Street: Congregational Church (right) and former Sandeman Library (left)

Between the two buildings runs Mill Street, and beyond the Library, the facades of Kinnoull Street and Scott Street lead into the distance. The church was built between 1897 and 1899, the memorial stone being laid by Mr John Moncrieff on 16th October 1897. It was opened for worship in April 1899. It cost £6,000. The architects were Steele and Balfour, Glasgow. See adjacent photograph for note on Sandeman Library.

The Murray Royal Hospital: Muirhall Road

The hospital was built in 1825-26 from a bequest of James Murray, a beneficiary under the will of his half brother William Hope who had perished at sea after amassing a large fortune in Madras, India. Under the trusteeship of David Beaton and Robert Peddie, James Murray's will to build an asylum for the insane came into being. The cost was £20,000. Under a Royal Charter dated 5th March 1827, signed by R. Peel, Home Secretary, the Institution was incorporated as "James Murray's Royal Asylum". (This document is carefully preserved in the archives of the Institution.) Now designated the "Murray Royal Hospital" it has carried out its founder's wishes and those of succeeding governments — both local and central — for over 150 years. Considerable recent additions include modern accommodation for psychogeriatric patients.

Architectural Note: The building was completed in 1826, the architect — Wm. Burn. North wings were added 1833, also by Wm. Burn. It is a plain neoclassic building in H plan with advanced wings to the north. It is of two-storey and basement design, built in whinstone ashlar with sandstone dressings. The south front has a five-window central pavilion, centre bay advanced, with coupled Roman Doric Porch, tripartite first floor window, octagon over, with bipartite windows and conical roof rising from behind parapet. It has long eight-window links to advanced two-window ends. The north front is three-storeyed in fall of ground to a five-bay frontage. There is a square glazed porch with fan tracery and plain parapet. Listed "B".

See also the detached Chapel. Listed "B".

The Chapel, Murray Royal Hospital
The entrance and tower.

The Chapel, Murray Royal Hospital

Built to the design, in late Scots Gothic, of Dr A. R. Urquhart, Physician Superintendent (1879-1913) who also designed the furnishings.

Architectural Note: The lower part, in whinstone rubble, was erected by the patients and workmen at the hospital under the supervision of Mr T. Whyte. The upper part is built in rock faced coursers with buttressed apse at the north-west. The tower at the south-east is in random rubble having crow stepped gable and an octagonal timber and lead cupola, this surmounted by an ornamental wrought iron weather vane. Listed "B".

Marshall Monument, Museum and Art Gallery

The monument was erected to Thomas Hay Marshall of Glenalmond, Lord Provost of Perth who did much to promote the advancement of the city and was the prime mover in the planning and erection of those grand embellishments to the city that we call collectively, Georgian Perth. Marshall was fortunate in acquiring the services of Robert Reid, later to become the king's architect, and their combined efforts at the turn of the 18th-19th centuries resulted in the erection of elegant terraces to the south and north of the town facing the respective Inches (q.v.). The citizens acknowledged his good works on behalf of the city and in gratitude caused the building of the rotunda and colonnade, here seen, as a memorial to him. Hence the words on the frieze — "Thomas Hay Marshall Cives Grati". The statue was added later.

Architectural Note: The design was by David Morison, an amateur, Secretary of the Literary and Antiquarian Society of Perth. It is strictly classical with Ionic columns. The use of Roman Ionic capitals with the volutes angled at 45° is unusual in 1827 when the Greek version with parallel volutes was the rule.

The **Art Gallery and Museum** were added 1932-35, the architects — Smart, Stewart and Mitchell. The entire collection of Natural history specimens of the Perthshire Society of Natural Science, carefully built up since its founding in 1867 was transferred to this new building. Similarly the library of reference books and other books on every branch of natural history was transferred and housed in a room of the new building, especially planned and built into the corporate design as the Library of the Perthshire Society of Natural Science. Hundreds of rare and valuable books are to be found there and can be viewed by special arrangement. Prior to 1935 the books and specimens were in the care of the Society in its own museum in Tay Street (q.v.).

Architectural Note: The museum and art gallery is single-storeyed with basement, is built in ashlar and has a large keystoned doorway with relief sculpture above. It has four windows to George Street, and has an Ionic-columned interior. In 1954 the dome of the rotunda was remodelled. Listed "B".

Tay Street: Nos. 56-72 (the southern end)

This row of buildings was erected prior to 1881 when the main section — the Museum of the Perthshire Society of National Science — was officially opened (1st October 1881). The architect was John Young. The various parts were: left to right — The Lodge of the Scottish Girls' Friendly Society, the Museum of the P.S.N.S., the Working Boys' and Girls' Hall and the corner building with Canal Street (with pyramid roof) which, although designed as an Opera House later became the Perth Baptist Church. It was destroyed by fire in 1984. An extension to the back of the museum was built in 1895. On the completion of the new museum and art gallery in George Street (q.v.) all specimens were removed there where they remain on display. The library of the P.S.N.S. was likewise transferred to a new library built for the society in the museum in George Street.

Architectural Note: A Romanesque building of Rhenish inspiration, characterised by long two-storeyed stugged coursers with four-storeyed corner having a pyramid roof. The frontage is punctuated by a gabled three-storey and attic tower near the south end, with a first floor oriel and two gabled, three-storey towers with pepper pots between and crow stepped gablets at sub-centres. It has a crow stepped centre gable in the Canal Street frontage. Listed "B".

The Marshall Monument (q.v.) and The Old Post Office, No. 80 George Street

The Marshall Monument is described under an adjacent photograph.

The old Post Office (right), the bowed section of which appears on an old map of 1784 was the home as well as the business premises of postmaster Charles Graham Sidey. His other business interests were stationer, bookseller and printer. As Lord Provost of Perth he welcomed Queen Victoria and Prince Albert on their visit in 1842. The Post Office appeared as an engraving on the cover of the Perth Post Office Directory of 1843, three years after the introduction of Rowland Hill's Penny Post. A copy of this original cover still exists. The building was the first of Perth's four main Post Offices in use over a period of a century and a half. It was succeeded by one at No. 2 High Street in 1862, a third in High Street in 1898 and the present G.P.O. in South Street in 1973.

Architectural Note: Built about 1784. A three-storey and basement building with a two-storey wing added later. Classic east front with a two-storey bow; Venetian window and pediment over. Listed "B".

Statue of Thomas Hay Marshall

Attributed to a local stone mason and sculptor called Cochrane, the statue stands behind the colonnade of the monument.

Art Gallery, Interior

The Ionic columned interior with Sculpture hall.

Sharp's Institution: Nos. 6 and 8, South Methven Street

Founded in 1860 by John Sharp, Barnhill.

According to Mr Sharp's Trust the Governors were enjoined to maintain the institution as a higher class school for boys and girls alongside Perth Academy. Significant intake was from the surrounding landward area.

At a cost of over £6,000 new chemistry and physics departments and an extended art department were opened in 1896, the design by Murray Robertson, Dundee. The institution was absorbed into Perth Academy when the Old Academy in Rose Terrace (q.v.) moved to Viewlands. The building was used as offices of the Tayside Regional Council from 1975 passing to the new Perth and Kinross Council in 1996.

Architectural Note: Stylish Italianate in design by David Smart (1824-1914) and built in 1860. Smart was a pupil of David Bryce and the style is to some extent a reflection of the latter's former surgical hospital (now the University's Natural Philosophy building) of 1848-53 in Edinburgh's Drummond Street.

Northern District School

Built in 1908 by the architect, G. P. K. Young. Sited on Dunkeld Road at the northern outskirts of Perth its function was to serve that area with its expanding population. The official opening was performed by Lord Shaw of Dunfermline on 29th August 1910.

Architectural Note: Edwardian Renaissance style, two-storey, red sandstone. Symmetrical fronts north-west and south-east. Double stepped north-west front has central entrance porch with tall arched window rising into segmental pediment above. Two cupolas with Ionic columns and weather vanes. Listed "B".

Perth Prison   ▷

The prison was built by Robert Reid in 1810-12 at a cost of £130,000 as a depot for 7,000 prisoners from the Napoleonic Wars. His plan was for four three-storey blocks radiating from a central court or marketplace where citizens could barter for toys and artefacts made by the prisoners.

The gatehouse, pictured here, was built at a time of reconstruction as Scotland's first general prison in 1839-42. The architect was Thomas Brown. Several buildings within the prison complex are listed; the categories being as follows:

A Block — "B"
H Block — "B"
Former governor's house — "B"

Former Surgeon's house — "C"
L Block — "B"
Gatehouse — "C"

Main Block — "B"
A and D Halls — "B"
Original Perimeter Wall — "B"

Architectural Note: The twin Military Walk buildings flanking the main entrance, the former Governor's House at 5 North Square, and L block (the former hospital) are the only parts of Robert Reid's P.O.W. prison to survive in their original condition. The central building in the prison forecourt lost its tall octagonal observation tower c. 1965. Reid's layout was quite different from the present, a D-arrangement with four blocks round the perimeter, open-plan with hammocks slung from cast-iron vertical tubes which were perforated for ventilation, and was based on the design of Daniel Asher Alexander's similar P.O.W. prison at Dartmoor. An inverted fortification wall enclosed a canal or moat — a renaissance fortress turned inside out. In 1839 Thomas Brown was instructed to rebuild it as Scotland's first general prison. Reid's barrack type blocks were demolished and the present five-armed radial layout of central chapel and four cell blocks begun. C and B halls, (the latter now demolished) were built in 1839-42 and A and D halls by the Government architect Robert Matheson in 1852-57. The original halls set the pattern of Scottish prison design for the remainder of the century although the Georgian-type radial layout was not repeated. An interesting circular exercise yard with a high iron perimeter fence survives south of C hall.

The Bell's Sports Centre

Gifted to the City of Perth by the Gannochy Trust as a memorial to A. K. Bell, founder of the Trust. Opened in 1968. Floor space is 32,000 sq. ft. Dome area 42,600 sq. ft. It was the largest dome in Europe at the time. Architect: J. B. Davidson of the Burgh Architects' Department. Cost: £225,000. Can accommodate all indoor sports and adaptations of some outdoor sports.

Fair Maid's House, Curfew Row

Sir Walter Scott's fictional "Fair Maid of Perth" was portrayed as having resided here in 1396. Her name was Catharine Glover, daughter of Simon Glover, deacon of the craft of Glovemakers. In 1629 (in truth) the Glovers' Incorporation of Perth bought the premises and used them as a meeting hall for over 150 years. Since 1968 they have been used as a craft and curio shop.

Architectural Note: A two-storey house incorporating mediaeval fragments. Most of the masonry was renewed and the interior restored in 1893-94: Architect, John Young. Rubble built with stair tower and slated roof. A niche in the corner, reputedly for a curfew bell, was probably for an image of St Bartholomew, patron saint of the Glovers. Above the entrance is their motto "Grace and Peace". Listed "B".

On the right stands the remains of the **Town House of Lord John Murray.** The main part, now demolished, stood behind in what was earlier the garden of the Blackfriar's Monastery. Lord John was the eldest son of the first Duke of Atholl and was M.P. for Perthshire 1734-61. He became Colonel of the Black Watch in 1745 and at the time of his death was senior officer of the Army.

Architectural Note: An 18th century, two-storey and attic building, rubble built. Has three-arched ground floor entries with in and out voussoirs. Five-window first floor and two small dormers. Listed "B".

97

H

Marshall Place and St Leonards in the Fields, Trinity Church ▷

Stunning sunsets over river and city are an uplifting feature during winter months

High Street, from the east   ▷

Kinnoull Church   ▷

The 'Fair' City added 'Floral' to its name in the nineties when it won both British and European awards. Kinnoull Church looks down.

Panorama of Marshall Place facing the Parklands of the South Inch.

Museum and Art Gallery, from Perth Bridge

◁ **Bridgend reflections**
The old houses of Commercial Street reflected in the river Tay at high tide. The warm Sunlight gives a hint of an Italian aspect to the scene. The buildings were demolished in 1975

◁ **Downstream from Queen's Bridge**
A young angler carefully positions himself to catch a trout.

Kinnoull Hill Tower at sunset ▷

IV. PRIVATE HOUSES

IN this section we show some representative examples of this type of building. All were built in the Georgian or Victorian period and the great majority are listed in the "B" category. Of the 16 houses selected only eight are still in use as family houses: three are hostels; two are Old People's Homes; one is in use as business premises; one is an Ex-Service Club, and one a Funeral Home. Their contribution to the architectural heritage of Perth, as with many others of their kind, is undisputed.

Craigie Park House, Craigie Road

This self-contained stone-built house has been occupied by the following since 1887 — Mr Kirkwood Hewat, Mr Robert c. Forbes and Dr Robert Buchanan. From 1931 and for a number of years it was Craigie Park Nursing Home. It is presently in use as children's nursery.

Architectural Notes: Early 19th century two-storey house with early 20th century extension. Built in black whinstone with sandstone dressings. Moulded arched doorpiece on east front. Later extensive alterations at south with outside stair to first floor and a single storey extension. Listed "C".

Ardchoille House: Strathmore Street

The house was the residence of the sixth Earl of Mansfield. He died in 1935. It was formerly named "Rosemount". Built about 1851 it is "Scots Baronial" in the style of Bryce's adherents. Probably Andrew Heiton's work. Is of irregular "L" plan with corbelled angle turrets and crow stepped gables. It became the H.Q. of Perth County Constabulary in 1954 and continued as H.Q. of the combined force till 1977. It is listed "B".

Springland, Isla Road

Built probably about 1790. During the 19th century was the home of Mrs Stewart-Sandeman who was the niece of the poetess Baroness Nairne (Caroline Oliphant of Gask).

Architectural Notes: A building of two-storeys with basement, three-windowed with gabled roof and angle urns: painted ashlar; Roman Doric porch, Ionic pilaster order with pediment above: canted bay through both floors to river. East addition and rear addition on 1808 map. Listed "B". The spring in the grounds is housed in a stone built wellhouse set in the slope of the ground. Rubble with two arched windows and centre door. Two stone vents for ventilation. Used for the cultivation of ferns.

▷

Springland, Fernhouse Well

Built into the slope of the ground around the spring this little feature in the garden resembles a shrine. Its moist, cool shade makes it conducive to the growth of ferns. Dated c. 1800. Listed "C".

Springland, Boathouse

Built about 1800 this boathouse, seen here on the bank of the River Tay with the house itself in the background, is described as a rubble built gazebo with crenellated parapet. The upper floor is reached by an outside stair on the landward side. Listed "B".

Bowerswell House, Kinnoull

Built in 1847 it was the home of the Melville Gray family who in 1855 referred to it as the "New House". Miss Effie Gray became the wife of John Ruskin, writer and foremost art critic of the time who lived with the Grays at Bowerswell, but after six years the marriage was annulled. In 1856 Effie married again, this time to John Everett Millais, an artist who was to become one of the founders of the pre-Raphaelite movement in art. The couple set up house at Annat Lodge (q.v.) where Millais painted what was later considered his finest work — "Autumn Leaves". Then after two years they moved to Bowerswell House. One of the works painted there was "The Vale of Rest" in which the background consisted of the view from the garden, and the foreground, of some of the stones in Kinnoull Churchyard. When still in his mid-30's he moved with his family to London where he already had a work base but returned to Scotland every year thereafter. His picture, "Chill October", painted at Kinfauns and admired by Van Gogh, hangs in Perth Art Gallery. Also, his series of paintings on the theme "The Parables of Our Lord" can be seen on the west window of Kinnoull Church (q.v.). He considered that mood was everything. Millais died in 1896 at the height of his career, having become President of the Royal Academy and a Baronet of the Realm — the first artist to be so honoured. He was buried in St Paul's Cathedral.

The Melville Grays continued to live at Bowerswell and as late as 1935 one of the last members of the family was prime mover in having a new carillon of bells installed in St John's Kirk.

Bowerswell House was taken over after the Second World War and converted for use as a War Memorial Home for the Aged. Officially opened in 1950 by Princess Margaret it consists of accommodation in the house for 20 residents and, in the grounds, a group of 20 cottages for couples.

Architectural Note: Built 1847, probably by Andrew Heiton & Son, it is in Italianate style, is two-storeyed in ashlar, is asymmetrical with three-storeyed entrance tower and finely detailed. It has an arched doorpiece with first-floor balustraded balcony over upon console-cantilever brackets and has a broad eaved, low pitched pyramid roof. The south-east front has asymmetrical gable with canted bay bearing consoled first floor balcony and cartouche over first floor window; south bay tripartite with cartouche at parapet: two canted bays at south-west front. North-west wing has consoled window and niche features. Square-shafted chimneys. Listed "B".

Hamilton House: Glasgow Road

Presently in use as a hostel by the Scottish Youths' Hostels Association. The house was built in 1865. The architect was Andrew Heiton. Owners included the Rev. Archibald Fleming of Inchyra for whom it was built, the Very Rev. Patrick Murray Smith, Provost of St Ninian's Cathedral, and later still, Lady Georgina Home-Drummond.

Architectural Note: Mid-Victorian Italianate style. Two-storey, ashlar. Main front to east. Central projecting gable with three-windowed cast iron balconied bow; three-storeyed tower in south; broad eaved low-pitched pyramidal roof; arched porch with balustraded parapet and urn in re-entrant angle of tower. Listed "B".

"Boatland," Isla Road

Early history is lacking but in present century Miss Marjorie Dence, co-founder and administrator of Perth Repertory Theatre, resided here for many years.

Architectural Note: An extraordinarily sophisticated house even by metropolitan standards. Early 19th century: two-storey and basement with broad eaved slated roof. On river front a three-window semi-circular bow. Handsome inside with rib vaulted entrance hall and oval staircase. Designer unknown. Listed "B".

"Tayfletts," Isla Road ▷

Attractively sited with green sward running down to the River Tay, this house was built probably at the turn of the 18th/19th centuries. It is rubble built with main block having two-storeys, attics, and wings.

Owners since 1900 included the following: Albert Evans Pullar, dyer; Mrs Clara Collins; Vice-Admiral Sir David Gregory; and Mr Ian MacArthur, M.P. Listed "B".

Annat Lodge, Kinnoull

Built probably in the latter part of the 18th century, Architect not known. Early owners included General Stuart, representative of the family Stuart of Annat in the Braes of Doune who were cadets of Ardvorlich, and he brought the name "Annat". Under General Stuart the house was restored by the architect Gillespie Graham in 1813. John Everett Millais and his wife Effie Grey (formerly Mrs John Ruskin) came to live here after their marriage and some of Millais's greatest pictures were painted here. Then in 1858-60 came George Payne Rainsford James, author and Consul General in Venice. Dr Buchanan White succeeded him and became the principal founder of the Perthshire Society of Natural Science in 1867. A recent owner was Charles D. Mactaggart who took over the house in 1958.

Kincarrathie House

The house was built on the estate which in 1755 belonged to Lieutenant Colonel James Sharp, Royal Perthshire Volunteers. His son possibly ordered its erection. It was enlarged in 1853 with the addition of a large bowfronted wing in 1922, A. K. Bell bought the house and after his death in 1942 the Gannochy Trust (his creation) added to it and converted it into an old people's home. Listed "B".

Cricket Pavilion: Do'cot Park

Erected to the order of Mr A. K. Bell of Kincarrathie House at the cricket ground he provided for residents of Gannochy Trust housing scheme. It is described as having two-storeys with log columns, an octagonal verandah and domical roof which is pantiled. Designed by Smart, Stewart & Mitchell in Arts and Crafts manner 1924-25.

"The Chapel," Kincarrathie House

This little building — quaint and picturesque — is said to have been built about 1694. It is situated on low ground to the east of the house, is darkly overgrown and now used as a garden shed. It is described as rubble built with two windows and centre door, gable front, gothic arched with ashlar dressings. Chimneys at rear. Listed "B".

Kincarrathie Do'cot

This is situated between the mansionhouse and the cricket pitch. It is described as follows: Rectangular lean-to, rubble with traces of harl. Inscribed "WSB:1SR:1694" at skews. There are two pigeon holes above the door. Listed "B".

Do'cots were the precursors of hen runs. They were widely distributed. Pigeon pie was never far down the menu in country houses.

Viewlands House, Viewlands Road

Residential Home run by the Abbeyfield Society Ltd, formerly used by the General Accident Assurance Corporation as a training centre for staff.

Architectural Note: Built c. 1840. Late classic villa. Two-storey, three-window, ashlar. Centre bay slightly advanced. Channelled ground floor. Central Ionic columned porch with balustraded parapet flanked by bay windows. Three architraved windows at first floor; main cornice and blocking course. Central bay has a balustraded parapet with supporting scrolls: Sphinxes over outer windows. Two dormers. Listed "B".

No. 10 St Leonard's Bank ▷

This is the last of the 10 detached stone-built villas built on high ground facing eastwards over the South Inch and numbering serially from King's Place. It is chosen as a representative example of the 10 which, although all are of similar size, they each have distinct differences in architectural features. They are all listed "B", except Nos. 1 and 2. No. 10 was built about 1835. The architect is not known. The entrance is on the south elevation having a Roman Doric porch, now unfortunately enclosed. There is a balustraded parapet at second-storey sections. It is presently in use as Royal Army Service Corps Club.

Architectural Note: Dr Adam Anderson, F.R.S.Ed and London, designed one of the 10 villas in St Leonard's Bank for his own use and continued occupancy until his death in 1846. He was rector of Perth Academy from 1809-37. During this period he also designed and supervised the building of the town's waterworks (q.v.) in Marshall Place — 1832. He followed Sir David Brewster in the chair of Natural Philosophy at St Andrews University.

Bellwood House, Dundee Road

Was the home of Archibald Turnbull, a textile factor. He formed a partnership with a Mr Dickson in a nursery business which became well known in Perth as Dickson & Turnbull. Two small cannon were mounted in front of the house at Bellwood. They were fired as the funeral cortege of Lord Lynedoch passed from Dundee to his last resting place in Methven. House unlisted.

No. 6 Kings Place

A house of individuality; quaint and attractive. Known but to a few it is tucked away in quiet seclusion. The architect and date of building are unknown but probably erected about 1845. Both the lancet Gothic windows and the weather-vane and dial are unusual in a single-storey and basement cottage house of that date. 1996: Further information supplied by an elderly local resident has it that the building was provided by the owners of Earlybank House as accommodation for domestic staff.

South Esk Bank: St Magdalene's Road

A house of individuality; quaint and attractive. Known but to a few it is tucked away in quiet seclusion. The architect and date of building are unknown but probably erected about 1845. Both the lancet Gothic windows and the weather-vane and dial are unusual in a single-storey and basement cottage house of that date.

"Glenshaugh," Bowerswell Road

Built c. 1845. Originally known as Gowrie Cottage.

Architectural Note: Single-storey with dormerless attic. L-plan harled and whitewashed; cantilever gable hood over doorpiece; bay window at Bowerswell Road gable, one attic window in Gowrie Street gable. Original glazing with wood centre mullions. Listed "B".

The "Old Presbytery": 26 Melville Street

Situated in back land in very confined space, this charming little building has been known but to a few since its erection, around 1840. Its features include semi-elliptically arched doorpiece and window, and crosslet crowstep gable at centre. Architect unknown. Listed "C".

V. CITY WALKABOUT

"TO get to know a place, explore it on foot." We have surely heard this advice often and may even have given it ourselves. As well as seeing at leisure what there is to see it is only on foot that we can detect the feel of a place. It is the advice we are going to follow in this section. We must bear in mind however that some retrospect will be necessary as the photographs are not all of the same period. Basically the streets and buildings are unchanged unless otherwise stated.

The walkabout takes in the following streets: Tay Street, South Street, Canal Crescent, South Street Port, County Place, South Methven Street, Atholl Street, Kinnoull Street, Murray Street, George Street, St John Street, St John's Place, Scott Street, Old High Street, and High Street.

9-11 High Street

Premises of the Royal Bank of Scotland.

Probably built about 1820. Peacock describes the building as it looked in the 1840's: "The branch office of the National Bank, near the bottom of the High Street, north side, is a fair substantial fabric, and marks itself out as a public office by four stately columns in front". This no doubt refers to the pilastered ground floor with central Doric columned doorpiece.

George Street: viewed from Watergate

Both sides of George Street are seen with the art gallery and museum as end point. The street came into prominence as the main approach way to the new Perth Bridge (1771). The buildings (q.v.) date from 1770 to the mid-19th century.

George Street: Nos. 5-21

From the pillar box on the east side of George Street there is an interesting variety of buildings within the space of a few yards.

Architectural Notes: Nos. 5-9 ("Hal o' the Wynd") late 18th century three-window with applied pilaster order and baroque architraves. Droved ashlar above.

Nos. 11-13 (A. T. Mays) late 18th century consoled ground floor shop. Three shouldered, architraved windows at first and second floors.

Nos. 15-21 ("Busy B" — Anderson's) mid-19th century three bays. Pilastered front; main cornice and balustrade. First floor group of three-stepped round arched windows with coupled pilasters each bay. Panelled spandrel areas. The buildings were converted into club rooms in 1887 by Andrew Heiton. All buildings listed "B".

Nos. 22 and 24 George Street

Basically of late 18th century design by Andrew Heiton & Son, refaced as an Italian mannerist palazzo with much rustication; for the Union Bank c. 1857-58.

High Street: Nos. 21-29

No. 21, Caird's, at corner of George Street, has the inscription 1774 on the gable facing into George Street. It is four-storeyed and is part of a larger building with a 12-window frontage. The top storey was at one time the home of Lord Provost David Ross, 1862-64. The shop was occupied by Messrs Wood, bakers from 1891-1970 and from 1971 by A. Caird & Son Ltd. It is listed "B" in a "B" group. Photo: May 1981.

High Street: north side, from No. 27

Taken in 1966 this view compares in part with the adjoining photograph taken 15 years later. Looking from right to left the sign "Groceries" is No. 27 and appears as "Victoria Wine" in 1981. Other local changes are evident but minor. This photograph gives clear evidence of the slight bend in High Street which we sometimes forget exists.

St John Street, Nos. 2-16

This photograph reveals some of the charm of Perth as a town of little shops — still noticeable in spite of modern trends. Many a passing stranger has been given cause to remember with pleasure the kindly reception given by assistants in such places. On one human contact can seem to depend the reputation of the city.

Architectural Note: Nos. 2-6, the corner building was built in the early 19th century. It is stuccoed with quoins and wallhead gable, has five windows to St John's Street and irregular fenestration to High Street. Is listed "B" in an "A" group.

Nos. 8-16, that part containing the Property Centre to Scott-Adie, inclusive, is also early 19th century in period. It has a six-window painted ashlar front. Is listed "B" in a "A" group.

On the left of the photograph, above "Thomas Cook", 25 High Street there appears part of the building cornering on George Street, dated 1774 on its gable (q.v.). It is stuccoed with ground floor shops and a 12-window frontage. It is listed "B" in a "B" group.

High Street, south side, from Kirkgate (left) to No. 76

The Victorian architecture of the upper storeys on right contrasts with the severe modern lines of the supermarket and cafeteria on left.

The buildings which are listed are as follows giving the name of the shop for easy identification:
No. 62, Slendos, listed "B".
No. 64, 66, K Shoes, listed "B".
No. 70, Close, listed "B".
No. 72, Allardyce, listed "B".
No. 76, Malcolm Campbell, No. 76 "C".
Photo: September 1980.

James McDonald, draper, 69 High Street

Part of the city scene in Perth for many years, McDonald's windows were noted for the large informative price ticket displayed on each item for sale. The "Retiral Sale" took place in 1958.

Nos. 75-81 High Street

These two shops, with Parliament Close between, were taken over and demolished in 1974 to make way for a new store of Marks & Spencer. Both were 18th century buildings but were unlisted. After demolition the cleared site was extensively investigated by Perth Archaeologists and many interesting and significant finds were made.

Corner Building: 104-112 High Street

Edwardian Renaissance in style: 1904. Menart & Jarvie, architects. Charles Jean Menart was Belgian born. He practised in Glasgow on his account as well as Perth. He specialised in R.C. Church architecture.

Architectural Note: Four-storey ashlar corner tower with canted bays first and second floors; Ionic segmentally pedimented aedicules third floor. Scroll supported octagonal drum and dome; longer facade to King Edward Street with central bay over doorpiece. Listed "A". On the left is seen the facade of the City's Guild Hall.

Mercat Cross, King Edward Street

This cross, seen against the frontage of the City Hall, was erected in 1913 as a memorial to King Edward VII. It is at least the fourth such cross in the city's history.

In early times the old Mercat Cross of a town marked the most public part from which all royal and public proclamations were made. There is no remaining record of such an early cross in Perth but one existed in the reign of James VI (1566-1625) at the intersection of High Street with Kirkgate and Skinnergate. In 1651 this cross, along with grave stones and stones from buildings demolished for the purpose, went into the building of Cromwell's Citadel on the South Inch. A third cross was erected in 1669, similar to the second. This eventually proved too great an obstruction to traffic anticipated by the use of the new Perth Bridge (built 1765-71) and it was removed. There was therefore no mercat cross in Perth between the years 1765 and 1913.

High Street looking west from King Edward Street (See next page.)

High Street: middle section of south side, looking eastwards

Compare with adjoining photograph. This overlaps and shows the facade as it stretches out towards the River Tay but is intersected by King Edward Street (at "Trueform"). The shop — "Wallace's" — at the near hand corner of King Edward Street was fated to be demolished in 1982 to make way for a superstore of the Fraser chain.

Note: High Street and South Street were the two main east west streets in medieval times. Mention is made of them as early as 1180. They were connected in the east, near the River Tay, by Watergate, and in the west by Meal Vennel.

High Street looking west from King Edward Street

(See previous page.)

These two photographs were taken about 12 years apart. The later one, of April 1982, shows scaffolding on the left following demolition of Wallace's store and adjoining shops (these all to be replaced by a new store of the Fraser chain). The other, earlier photograph shows Wallace's and adjoining shops as they were in the sixties, and further west the G.P.O. building which was demolished in 1973. Also note the distant cupola on right on the Royal Bank building at the corner of Methven Street. This was removed in 1971.

High Street, middle section of south side, looking westwards, 1979

Marks & Spencer's building shown here, was erected 1961-63 on a site which included the Bluebell Close at No. 136. Also shown are shops of John Menzies, which, with Marks & Spencer were soon to be moving to new sites nearer the River Tay on the opposite side of High Street. Charles Rattray, tobacconist, was to close down; Williamson, funeral director, to move to other premises; John Collier to close down and the old roadway — Meal Vennel — which is seen between John Menzies' shop and Terley's, was under threat of closure to traffic.

The building with the cast iron cresting is at the corner with Scott Street.

Rattray's Tobacconist, High Street   ▷

The firm of *Charles Rattray*, tobacco manufacturer occupied the premises at 160 High Street from c. 1915 until 1981. The history of the building as a tobacco curing and blending business goes further back than this being under the name of A. Thomas Paterson in the 1890's and Brown and Rattray at the turn of this century.

Mr Rattray specialised for many years in trade signs for snuffs and tobaccos — especially "Figures" such as West Indians, sailors, Highlanders, Turks — building up one of the best collections in the country.

The special "atmosphere" within the spacious and finely fitted premises was successfully retained right up until its closure in April 1981. Most of the fittings were then removed to Perth Museum for safe preservation and display. (See next page.)

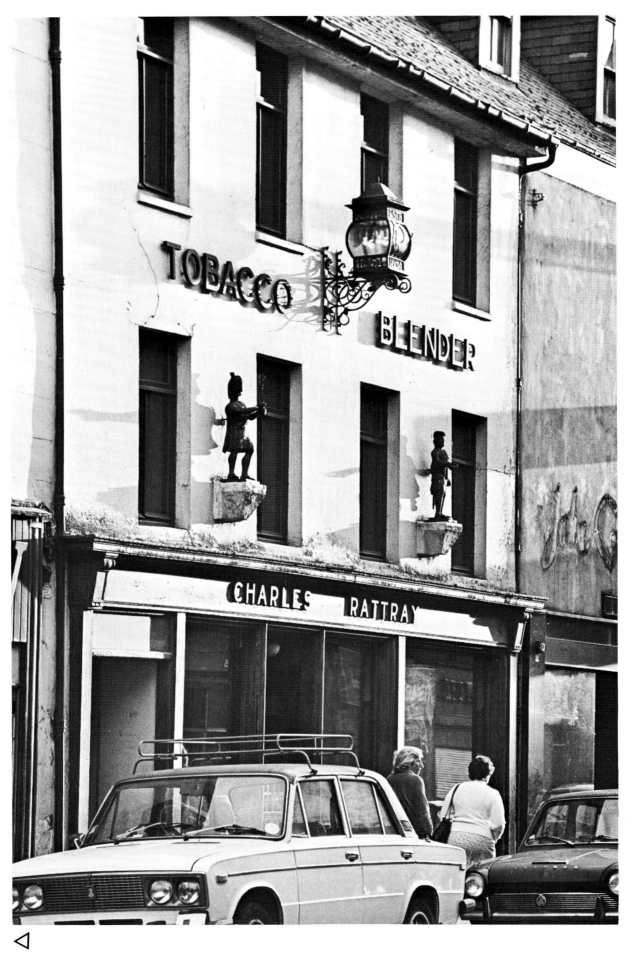

High Street: north side, from Wm. Watson's westwards

As seen in 1978. The building containing Nos. 177-187 High Street (i.e. with shops — Light Bite; Maypole; Perth Theatre and Weir) is listed "B". Perth Theatre designed by William Alexander, City Architect of Dundee and the local theatre specialist at that date is of special interest. The foyer is glass roofed with decorative cast iron trusses. It contains a bronze portrait relief of Miss Marjorie Dence, who was co-founder, with David Steuart, of Perth Repertory Theatre. This was unveiled in 1969: the artist was Mr Scott Sutherland. The auditorium of the theatre is of horse-shoe plan, the circle and balcony being supported on cast iron columns; the ceiling is circular. It was first opened on 6th September 1900, the proprietor and manager being J. H. Saville (d. 1924). The repertory theatre was formed in 1935. Modernisation has been done in stages, notably in 1967 and 1982. The District Council takes an active part in the running of the theatre.

G.P.O. Corner: High Street/Scott Street ▷

This photograph taken before 1960 shows Perth's favourite trysting place on a Saturday afternoon. Note the ladies' fashions. A short step into the '60's will take them into the dress revolution of the mini skirt. The buildings in the background, whilst the upper storeys show little change in 25 years, the shops below have all changed in ownership and pursuit. The block containing Nos. 177 to 187 High Street, i.e., MacFisheries, Perth Theatre and Maypole, is listed "B". (See foot of next page.)

Pullar's Corner — Kinnoull Street/Mill Street

The firm of *J. Pullar & Sons Limited,* cleaners and dyers, was founded by John Pullar in 1824 at the head of Burt's Close — situated between 129 High Street and 19 Mill Street.

Originally he concentrated on dyeing yarn from his father's handloom factory and from local yarn firms — soon moving on to fabric and silk dyeing.

Amalgamations with Eastman's of London and Messrs P. & P. Campbell of Perth followed and by the time the firm celebrated its 100th anniversary it was employing 2,500 at Perth and 1,500 more directly throughout the country.

By the 1930's the original buildings had undergone many alterations and other buildings had been "adapted" — including three churches, two schools, a gasworks, tavern and a snuff-mill, in order to keep up with the firm's rapid expansion.

In 1930 — a quarter of a million customers sent articles direct to Perth by post and hundreds of thousands used the 150 branches and 4,000 agents.

By the 1970's with most articles being dry-cleaned on the branch premises, the need for the vast Mill Street complex had passed, and sections of it were subsequently sold off. Recipients included the District Council and, most recently a supermarket chain.

Architectural Notes: Good simple industrial Victorian Renaissance at the broad eaved pedimented sections. Architect not known but comparable in merit with the better Dundee jute mills. Listed "B".

Kinnoull Street/Scott Street Facade

This shows the low even numbers of Kinnoull Street starting from the left at No. 2 (Provincial Building Society) which is listed C and Nos. 6-12 (Royal Insurance — McCash & Hunter) — Listed C. David Smart was architect of both, the corner building in 1900 and Nos. 6-12 in or about 1905.

Architectural Note: Nos. 2 and 4 Kinnoull Street; otherwise known as Royal Bank Building (q.v.) and seen here with the sign "Provincial Building Society" was designed by David Smart in late Victorian Renaissance style. It is three-storeyed with attic in red ashlar. It features a three-bay frontage and splayed one-window corner, arched ground floor, arched doorpiece in Ionic aedicule with curved pediment at corner: fluted corinthian pilasters first and second, pedimented first floor windows, centre window columned; pavilion roof with pedimented dormers, bracketed cornice with balustraded parapet. Listed "C".

Nos. 6-12 Kinnoull Street was built five years later (1905). The style was similar but with different floor levels providing four-storeys. Listed "C".

High Street from Old High Street

This is the prospect as seen from Old High Street at the junction of New Row. The westering sun brings out detail and texture on the buildings. The Old High Street Port was situated at the level of St Pauls' Church (right). We look past this straight into High Street as far as the corner of Scott Street where the corner building is marked by its cast iron cresting. The truncated cupola of the Royal Bank building is seen on the left.

Note on St Paul's Church: One of the city churches, St Paul's was built in 1807, the architect being John Paterson. The style is Baronial Gothic. In form it is a crenellated octagon with outshots to east, west and south; the tower with spire is on the north side and has a gable and belfry stage and diagonal pinnacles. The building is in ashlar and the angles of the outshots are shafted and have pepperpots. Listed "B".

Peter Thomson, High Street

The closing-down sale in 1973 brought crowds in search of bargains. The business traded from the year 1908 as a high-class grocer and wine and spirit merchant. But after this and other retail outlets closed, the business concentrated on whisky blending and wine importing and distributing.

Kinnoull Street/High Street Crossing

This crossing could claim to be the "City Centre" on grounds of both geography and business activity. The latter however has tended in recent years to gravitate to the lower part of High Street and St John's Street. The handsome building facing us is seen to assume a self importance in stance and bearing, fully intended by the architect, to match its central site. The architecture — David Smart's work — has been described under an adjoining photograph. Listed "C".

High Street Port: 1973

At the west end of High Street at its crossing with South Methven Street there was situated a gate or port in the old city wall. A branch of the mill lade — the canal — passed close by on its way along the line of South Methven Street to Canal Crescent and Canal Street. St Paul's Church which we see here was built (1806-7) on the site of a landing stage on the canal. Beyond the port the houses of Old High Street can be seen disappearing in the distance. The gate was removed about 1764 and by 1790 the city wall had been levelled.

Covering the Town's Lade: Mill Street, 1953 ▷

Manpower in use for moving concrete sections into place over the lade. The area is now a car park lying between Mill Street and Murray Street. In this picture the buildings of South Methven Street (left) and North Methven Street (right) are seen in shadow in the middle distance; whilst beyond these, at the end of West Mill Street, the gable end of the upper city mill is seen breaking the skyline. Picture is from a damaged negative rescued from oblivion.

Frontage of Murray Street

The buildings of Murray Street make a rather haphazard assortment when viewed from west Mill Street. They range in period over a century and a half. Pullar's chimney seen in the centre of picture was demolished in October 1980. Photograph: 1977.

South Methven Street west side

The buildings on the west side of South Methven Street are on the right when looking southwards to South Street Port. This latter is marked by the traffic signals. The pedimented building designated "Alexander and Brown" — Nos. 61 to 71 — dates from about 1840. Late classic in design. Central first floor window and end windows of flanking are consoled and pedimented. Listed "B". Photo 1977.

△
◁

South Methven Street east side: 1950-80

Compare these two photographs, 30 years apart in time, using the chemist's pestle and mortar sign on the right as key. Notice that the upper storeys and dormers are virtually unchanged but on the other hand almost all of the shops have changed in ownership and pursuit. One exception is worthy of special mention — the chemist, R. P. Blair — successfully updated with paint only.

The building with central pediment and vermiculated rustication between shops (i.e. from "R. P. Blair" on right to "Licensed Restaurant" on left, inclusive) and with six canted dormers, is listed "C".

139

South Street Port and South Methven Street from King Street

South Methven Street runs into the distance on the left of the picture, whilst the buildings in the centre and right, at the corners of South Street, are those described in the adjoining picture. King Street, from which the picture was taken runs southwards from the port to the South Inch.

County Place

Taken from South Street Port in 1979 this photograph shows plainly the diversity of design in shop fronts. Perth has always been a town of little shops, to which feature at least some of its charm must be attributed. "The Corner Shop" is listed "C".

◁ ## South Street Port

From a viewpoint at the west end of South Street — otherwise known as South Street Port — we look into County Place (right) which leads to Glasgow Road, and on the left into Hospital Street which leads to Leonard Street and Perth Railway Station. The gushat building in the centre of the picture consists of Nos. 2, 4, 6 and 8 County Place on the right and 1, 3 and 5 Hospital Street on the left. It is listed "B". On the extreme left is King James VI Hospital (q.v. listed "A"), under restoration at the time of photograph, 1974.

Historical Note: South Street Port (or "South Gait Port", in the old vernacular) was an entrance to the town for travellers from the south and west in mediaeval times. The Edinburgh and Stirling roads converged near the port; but from 1770 onwards the new Edinburgh Road via Princes Street and the South Inch came into use leaving the Port as the main south-westward approach, i.e. from Stirling and Glasgow. (See previous page.)

South Street: the north side in 1978

Taken looking eastwards, the buildings in this photograph compare with those on the adjoining one, taken c. 25 years earlier (with cyclists). Changes in the shop fronts are evident. None of the buildings seen is listed.

South Street Port and South Street from County Place

Looking down South Street towards the River Tay and beyond where the tree clad slope of Kinnoull Hill can be seen, the corner buildings at the Port stand out prominently. The one on the left — "the Central Bar" — No. 189 South Street was designed by McLaren & MacKay in Edwardian Renaissance style and built in 1900-01. Note the three-window corner octagon bay with corbelled Ionic columns, also the pyramidal roof. It is listed "B". On the right the corner block is now a bank, designed by Dunn & Findlay of Edinburgh in the Edwardian Free Renaissance style and built in 1903-4. Note the circled three-window corner with broad eaved ogee roof. Listed "B".

◁ ## Cyclists, South Street

With no worries about one-way streets or double yellow lines this group of young cyclists stop off in South Street for a brief stay. The time was the mid-50's when Perth was usually considered by travellers as a place that had to be traversed to get to somewhere else. Compare the buildings on left of the photograph with those on the photograph above it, taken 25 years later, using the corner building in centre as key.

Canal Crescent

The Crescent followed a line parallel to the old canal as it emerged from the direction of South Methven Street and, describing a quarter circle, straightened into the line of Canal Street and then flowed onwards to the River Tay. The photograph was taken from Canal Street looking (against the flow) along the Crescent.

North St John's Place

This shows the facade as it appeared in September 1973. The building with Nos. 5, 6, 7 and 8 (ref. right to left: "Ring o' Bells" to "McKillop, carpets") is early 19th century with shops and two upper floors, each with four windows. Listed "C". The building next in line, with Nos. 9 and 10 (right to left: "Kirkside Bar" to "Upholsterers") is late 18th century and has two upper storeys with five windows. Listed "B". Those buildings seen farther to the left: viz. Thomas Love & Sons (with tower), Scott's and Grants' are later buildings and are unlisted.

Lindsay's Garden Centre, 71 South Street

A long–established business which closed in 1994. It was a feature of the townscape scene in Perth, familiar to more than one generation of citizens. It closed down in 1994.

Stewart's Brushworks, 59 South Street

The inscription tells its own tale — "Established over 100 years". One of a number of small manufacturing businesses to close down in the 'sixties and 'seventies. A wide range of brushes of traditional design and specialist use were manufactured on the premises.

South Street: north side: Nos. 25-51

On this photograph the numbers run from right to left, the stretch being from St John's Street (right) to Fleshers' Vennel (Thomas Love & Sons) on left. That part towards the right (Nos. 29-37) having pilastered ground floor shops and central three-bay pediment above, was built about 1825, and occupies the site of the pre-reformation grammar school of Perth. An inscription on the central blind window reads as follows:

"The grammar school of Perth stood on the site of this building.

The Admirable Crichton is said to have been taught in this school.

The school was demolished by Cromwell in 1652 and rebuilt in 1773.

It was transferred to Perth Academy in 1807 and the old buildings were converted into a theatre in 1810-19. Burned in 1823.

St Anne's Chapel was situated between the school and St John's Kirk."

Nos. 43-51 South Street (Fisher's to Thomas Love & Sons: right to left) is dated about 1835 and having an eight-window front in ashlar with tripartites at No. 47, is listed "B" as also is the grammar school block above.

South Street: as viewed from Watergate

As seen on a bright April day in 1981. The traffic is heading for Queen's Bridge, 100 yards behind the camera. The building with the name Watergate and having a three-window front to South Street is listed "B". Behind it was situated the house of the Bishops of Dunkeld (see "Fountain Close").

A. S. Deuchar, 12 South Street

The name Deuchar has been associated with the antique trade in Perth for many years. Branches of the family had divergent interests. The old bow window here seen is the last surviving example in the city. It has now in 1984 been repaired and repainted.

Part of Tay Street from west end of Queen's Bridge

Nos. 36 to 44, seen on right, are otherwise known as Victoria Buildings. Designed by Andrew Heiton, 1872 in a Greek Revival manner of Thomsonesque type, it has slightly angled frontage with four pedimented tripartite bays, also pedimented doorpieces with incised ornament. Listed "B".

Nos. 46 to 52 (Gowrie House) was probably also designed by Andrew Heiton, in 1865-70. Built in French Gothic style it is an office building with symmetrical front and segmentally arched openings on ground floor, hood moulded, and bracketed with iron balustrated balconies. Gabled dormers. Listed "B". St Matthew's spire on right.

Tay Street from Dundee Road

The young trees in the foreground lead the eye upwards to the dignified frontage of Tay Street with the County buildings (q.v.) as focal point. The River Tay runs between. Other buildings are, on left, Baptist church with pyramidal roofed tower (destroyed by fire in 1984) and on the right the fiscals' office and Gowrie House (q.v.). Queens's Bridge is just visible through the foliage. Photo: May 1981.

Atholl Street: Nos. 9-17

This stretch of Atholl Street catches the eye with its profusion of architectural features. It is stylistically mid-19th century in period but Nos. 11-17 were probably in existence by the beginning of the century and altered later.

Architectural Note: No. 9, with No. 52 Kinnoull Street is built in ashlar with rusticated ground floor and has a segmentally arched doorway with fan light. There are five tall architraved windows to Atholl Street and three segmentally pedimented set-back dormers. Listed "B".

Nos. 11-17 have a 10-window frontage with square leaded windows on ground floor and two double pedimented doorpieces. The first floor windows have corbels under sills and wrought iron balconies at bipartites over door pieces. The second and fourth windows are slightly advanced and pedimented, the sixth, seventh, eighth, ninth and tenth have pedimented dormers over. The eighth has a small belfry feature. Listed "B".

Further to the right on the photograph, St Andrews Church can be seen and on the extreme right, St Ninian's Cathedral.

VI.   VIEWS AND VISTAS

VIEWS of townscapes are often best obtained from a high point either on the outskirts of the town or from a high building within the town. In the latter instance a series of shots are required to cover the areas around the building. Occasionally a vista at ground level can be effective. One's orientation can be greatly assisted by studying a good detailed photograph; our preconceptions can often be wrong.

View northwards from Railway Bridge over Tay

The clean lines of Queen's Bridge contrast with the traditional arches of Perth Bridge as we view these structures from the walkway on the railway bridge. The spire of St Matthew's Church dominates the scene. It is perhaps the most conspicuous landmark in the city.

Panoramic view northwards from Norie Miller Walk

In morning sunshine, Tay Street is seen on left, Perth Bridge in centre and the Norie Miller Riverside Walk on right.

April Prospect, North Inch

Drifts of daffodils lead the eye to Charlotte Street and Kinnoull Hill in the distance.

East Bridge Street — Lochie Brae

From the brae, at its narrowest, the view as seen on a summer evening in 1974. Sunshine from the north-west floods the buildings of Back Wynd and Potterhill Lodge, while in the distance the spire of St John's Kirk breaks through the skyline. In the foreground a housewife trudges uphill with her shopping. The wall on the right is that of Tayhill and on the left, Potterhill.

White Gables: Commercial Street

These three gables were for generations the focal point of the riverside view of Commercial Street. They are here seen from the North Inch in a frame of one of the arches of the bridge. High tide on the river and a low sun provide attractive reflections.

Perth from Cavendish Avenue

This vista from Cavendish Avenue, near its junction with Murray Crescent, leads downhill to the city centre where the spires of St John's Kirk (left) and nearby St Matthews (right) are clearly seen. The Pomarium Flats rise in front of the spires and in the far distance Murrayshall Hill (left) and Deuchney Hill (right) lie in shadow.

Prospect from East Bridge Street

The time of photograph was September 1980. Had it been one month later the tall chimney on right at Pullar's dyeworks would have vanished. It was demolished in October. The hoarding on the left conceals the site of the Back Wynd triangle (q.v.) which was demolished earlier in the year. At the far end of the bridge there are the old post office with pedimented gable and adjoining it on left the rotunda of the Marshall Monument and Art Gallery (q.v.). On the skyline on right beyond Pullar's chimney there is Perth High School and in centre the tower of Perth Academy. The Riverside Inn, seen on the left, is of particular interest. For centuries it was known as the "Cross Keys", this having succeeded an ancient hospice run by the monks of Scone Abbey: hence the Cross Keys sign of St Peter. The building of Perth Bridge which was completed in 1771 increased trade as the inn was on the main coaching route to the north and east. In 1836 the innkeeper, Mr Joseph Clark, had stabling for nearly 200 horses. The name "Clark's Close" survived until demolition of old Commercial Street (1975) as a narrow passage running from the Street to the River Tay.

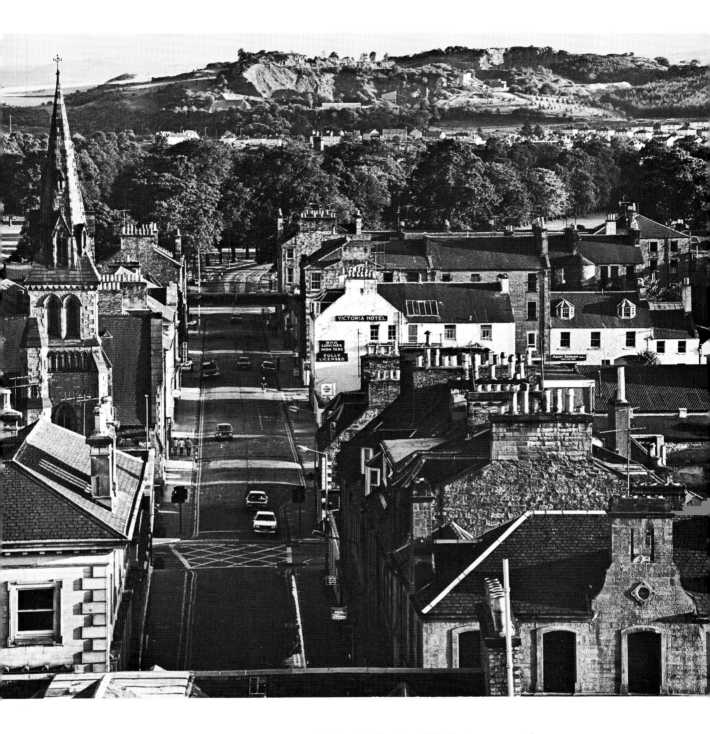

View from Tower of St John's Kirk to south

Looking south along the length of Princes Street the trees of the South Inch come into view as the street leads into the avenue through the Inch. Beyond the trees the houses of Craigie (right) and Friarton (left) lie spread out. More distant still is Perth quarry. The spire in the foreground on left belongs to St John's Episcopal Church. The buildings in the immediate foreground face onto South Street.

View from Tower of St John's Kirk to north

In the centre foreground we see Kirkgate running straight to the north. At the point where it reaches High Street (where the pedestrians are seen) there was situated the Old Cross of Perth. Beyond this is Skinnergate, still leading to the north and what was the old Dunkeld Road. Near the top of the picture the dome of the Marshall Monument, at the Perth Museum, stands out clearly and on the left of it the broad acres of the North Inch with cricket ground. Photo: 1960.

View from the Tower of St John's Kirk to west   ▷

The expansive view here includes on the left, foreground, the roof of the City Hall and above it the Central District School, then passing to the right, the spire of St Paul's Church at High Street Port, and right again, the cupola of the old G.P.O. at the corner of High Street and Scott Street. The skyline on the right is broken by three chimney stacks — all now demolished. St Ninian's Cathedral is seen on the extreme right. The hills in the distance lie above Crieff and the Sma' Glen. Photo. 1960.

View from Tower of St John's Kirk to north-east

The spire of St Matthew's Church immediately claims the attention looking to the north-east. In the foreground the white facade of St John Street is seen and on the left, with cupola, the former headquarters of the General Accident Assurance Corporation. Above this on the photograph are the Potterhill Flats, and stretching to the right, the houses of the Kinnoull area, interspersed among the trees.

◁ *View from Tower of St John's Kirk to south east*

Looking over the rooftops of South Street the River Tay is seen flowing to the right, i.e. southwards. The spire of the Baptist Church, Canal Street, stands out boldly on the right. Beyond the River Tay, the white frontage of Hillside Homes is seen towards the left of the picture and beyond it the houses and parkland of Barnhill.

Kinfauns Castle

Gives focus to the varying landscape patterns as viewed from the southern slopes of Kinnoull Hill. Romantically situated, the castle was designed by Sir Robert Smirke and built between 1820 and 1822 to the commision of Francis 14th Lord Gray. Later, the castle was owned by the 17th Earl of Moray.

◁ *View from Tower of St John's Kirk to south west*

A church spire dominates the scene — that of St Leonards in the Fields (q.v.). The roofs in the foreground are those of the old houses in South Street and Canal Street while in the background the houses of Craigie and High Craigie can be seen (left). Craigie Hill rises behind on the right and Kirkton Hill on the left. The latter is locally known as Caller Fountain Hill.

M

From Kinnoull Hill, looking to Kinfauns Castle

Views like this have made Kinnoull Hill the favourite haunt of many of our citizens and one of the city's principal tourist attractions. For the expenditure of a little energy in a pleasant walk to the top the rewards are manifold. Around all the points of the compass, as viewed from the excellent indicator, skylines as far as Norman's Law in the east to Ben More and Stobinean in the west and Schiehallion, Ben y Gloe and the Cairnwell in the north can be easily seen.

The tower on the hill was erected by an Earl of Kinnoull as a pseudo-Rhenish ruin to enhance (with some success) the resemblance of the Tay to the Rhine at this point — landscape gardening on a grand scale. Kinfauns Castle can be seen to the right of the cliff.

Kinnoull Hill and The River Tay
This view from Kinnoull Hill, described by many as the finest in the district, never tires. It attracts walkers, from home and abroad, in all seasons of the year

Branklyn Pathway
Branklyn Garden. A flowery way — one of many — leads to Branklyn House.

Perth Bridge from the Royal George Hotel
Showing some buildings of Bridgend, and the fast flowing river Tay.

Tay Street from Queen's Bridge, winter
An early fall of snow outlines trees, buildings and, on the right, part of Perth Bridge.

Rose Terrace

The disciplined architecture of a Georgian Terrace is nowhere better exemplified than in Rose Terrace. The Old Academy, with Britannia aloft, provides a fitting centre piece

Part of Tay Street as seen from Perth Bridge   ▷

On the left, the Spire of St Matthew's Church, in the centre the former head office of the General Accident Assurance Corporation and on the right, part of the Perth District Council Chambers. In 1996, the General Accident Building is now in use as the Perth and Kinross Council Chambers and Offices. The River Tay runs southwards, to the left, in the foreground.

Perth Bridge and the North Inch

From the lower slopes of Kinnoull Hill, as seen through a long lens.

Cityscape of Perth using a long lens from Kinnoull Hill
Note Dewar's bonded store, now demolished

◁ ## *Rafts of Ice*
A winter scene from Perth Bridge. Rafts of floating ice build up near Stanners Island

◁ ## *PROTECTION*
Statue by Ronald Rae, at the entrance to headquarters of General Accident Assurance Corporation.

St John's Kirk   ▷
Spire in sunshine and Halkerston Tower in shade.

VII. SOME NOOKS AND CRANNIES

THE countryside has its lanes and byeways where few strangers penetrate. Cities have their lanes and back alleys known but to a few. Perth has its closes and vennels. This section explores a few of them and focuses on a number of surprises — some significant, some just quaint. They add yet another dimension to heritage.

Back stairs, Reform Place

That part of Canal Street between Scott Street and James Street was known as Reform Place. Behind Nos. 84-100 the back stairs produce an interesting pattern when viewed from an end window. The houses, said to have been tenanted by sailors who crewed the ships of Perth, appear on the map of the town of 1837, i.e. five years after the passing of the Reform Act of 1832.

Open "All Hours"

"Curio Shop", 86 Canal Street. Established by Mr I. C. Imrie in the late '60's, this was one of several antique shops that opened up locally during a resurgence of the trade. This augmented the well-established reputation of Perth as an antique centre in mid-Scotland.

Incorporation of Wrights: Door in Watergate

By 1949 the *Wright Incorporation* consisted of seven "sciences" — wrights, barbers, coopers, slaters, plasterers, glaziers and masons. (Formerly also included surgeons and bookbinders). At this time members of the Incorporation were very tenacious of their rights and privileges and often raised prosecutions against individuals for doing private jobs.

The ornamental doorway was gifted as a gesture of thanks and goodwill by masons who had been given the use of the hall at a time when their own hall was unusable. Hence the mason's emblem above the door.

166

No. 27 Watergate: pedimented doorpiece

Dated 1725 this doorway leads to part of the building formerly owned by the Wrights' Incorporation and is the third door to the south of the main entrance to the Wrights' Hall at No. 23 (q.v.). Along with the latter doorpiece it is described as Artisan Renaissance in style. The building which is three-storeyed, stuccoed and with ten windows is now converted to business premises. The last meeting in the hall was in 1968.

Spiral Stairway to Wrights' Hall

At No. 23 Watergate this spiral stairway led to the Wrights' Hall on the first floor. Note the square iron frame for a lamp. Also note the hardwood handrail, no doubt made by a master of the craft to the highest standards at all times aware of the appraising eye and the critical hand of his peers on their upward way to the Deacon's Court. The building was gutted and rebuilt internally c. 1980. Photographed 1968.

Wrights' Hall: interior

Shows deacon's chair, table and chairs of clerks. Behind is the highly decorated pew front with insignia which is now to be seen in St John's Kirk.

Incorporation of Wrights: Deacon's Chair

This can now be seen in Perth Museum, George Street.

169

Perth Foundry

The foundry was started up by a firm, Alexander McFarlane & Co., in 1820. It was situated in Paul Street where the accompanying photograph was taken at the end of 1969, shortly before it was closed down. It had been run by Messrs Robertson & Robertson since 1901. The new foundry is at Ladeside, St Catherine's Road. Their products include gravity die and sand castings and they also manufacture pattern dies and moulds.

◁ ## St Matthew's Hall and Church Officer's House

At No. 34 Watergate, across the courtyard behind St Matthew's Church, there is to be found this quaint and interesting building. It is the old hall of the church — the "Free West Church Mission Hall" — now superceded by a much larger hall with better appointments. The upper part contains the Church Officer's House. Originally an 18th century building it was much reconstructed in the early 19th century and altered again by J. Honeyman in 1871. It is two-storeyed in rubble with stair tower. The ground floor was reconstructed to the hall. It has three arched windows, one square-headed; has three dormer heads and a corbelled feature to the north. Listed "C". As previously stated St Matthew's was the name given to the West Church on its being joined by the Middle Kirk, the Wilson Church and Bridgend Church in 1965.

Pend entrance: South Street

This pend led to the workshops of C. Smith & Son, joiners, on the south side of the street. It disappeared with the demolition of the building, including adjacent shops, in December 1983.

Handrail, common stair, 30/32 Caledonian Road

This photograph, taken on 25th September 1973 during the demolition of this tenement building not only records a feature of the building but also an example of workmanship worth noting. The handrail — much·used and no doubt much appreciated during its long life — has been unusually fashioned, giving due attention to height, girth and curve, to give maximum assistance to the ascending resident.

Corner of a back court: South Street

Note the outside stair to dwelling house; the upstand water supply; the drain; and the door to the outside w.c. All were surviving examples of domestic services in use in the 19th and early 20th centuries. Demolished, December 1983.

Ropemaker's Close, South Street

The close, so narrow as to be almost claustrophobic, ran southwards for about 100 yards to Canal Street. It was one of several convenient short cuts for pedestrians crossing the city in a north/south direction. The height of the close as it passed through the building became reduced as a result of the levelling up of South Street. Ropemakers used it as a ropewalk during the twisting operation. By 1982 it had ceased to exist through demolition of neighbouring buildings.

Fleshers' Instruments in Relief

High on the wall of the Fleshers' building in South Street near its junction with Princes Street this relief is to be seen. Carved out of red sandstone the detailed rendering of the instruments leaves little doubt as to their purpose.

E.R. VIII

The year 1936 gives the clue to this insignia on the Employment Exchange in Alexandra Street. King Edward VIII acceded to the throne on the death of his father King George V in December of that year but abdicated before the coronation could be carried out.

Two centuries of service

Exposed to view after two centuries (on the occasion of adjacent demolition) this decrepit old building in South Street just holds together and no more. Heritage has many faces.

175

Old doorway, Albert Close

Another passageway, narrow and with a double angle, Albert Close, runs between George Street and Skinnergate. In it, this old doorway, complete with top-half shutters and wrought iron handrails still exists. It is but a few feet from the town's lade.

36 George Street ▷

Entrance to the Glovers' Hall is by way of this stair which can be seen with a sideways glance from the pavement. The building is late 18th century, four-storeyed, with four windows in the frontage. It has two canted dormers. Listed "C". The previous Glovers' meeting place was for a time in what we now know as the Fair Maid's House (q.v.).

Window: late 18th century

This old sashed window (one of several removed during alterations at Nos 86-102 High Street in 1979) showed some of the flaws inherent in the glassmaking process of the time. At top centre, bull's eye which occurred when the cooling glass, on gaining viscosity, failed to spread when dropped on the flat surface. The curving refraction patterns around this can be seen in the second row (right), and bottom (left). Bubbles of trapped air are present inn centre pains in second and third rows.

Architectural Notes: Early window pains were cut from glass crowns which originated in the Levant in the 14th century. A paraison or glass ballon was blown to begin with and this was cut across whilst it was kept spinning over a flat surface until it spread out into a large disc. When detached from the blowing iron a rough knob remained in the centre. Rectangular window pains were cut to size from the disc, the centre one including the knob or "Bull's Eye". The concentric ripples seen in old window pains were a sure sign of crown origin. There was always considerable distortion of both the transmitted image and the image reflected from the surface.

Fountain Close: 17 South Street ▷

The close, seen here occupied by a squad of young painters, was the entrance to the town house or palace of the Bishops of Dunkeld. The house backed on to Watergate. As a project by the pupils of Kinnoull School, seen here, the close was cleaned and painted with murals depicting the palace. In the absence of old plans or other visual records of the building full play of the imagination was allowed. Advisers were: Class teacher, Miss R. Fothergill, and artist: Mr A. W. Robson: The year: 1975.

Historical Note: Bishops Thomas Lawdor and Gavin Douglas were two of the incumbents in the 15th century. The following inscription appears in a blind window in St John Street:

"The house of the Bishops of Dunkeld stood behind these buildings in a garden bounded by Baxter's Vennel and entering from Fountain Close, South Street. This house was built prior to 1421." Gavin Douglas, Bishop of Dunkeld 1474-1522: "In a barbarous age gave to rude Scotland Virgil's page."

Hal o' the Wynd's Close: Mill Wynd

Mill Wynd runs from Old High Street to the Lower city mill. One of the buildings in the Wynd became identified as the house of Hal o' the Wynd, one of the principal characters in Scott's *Fair Maid of Perth*. The character and the association were, of course, fiction but the romance of Sir Walter seemed, to many, more acceptable than truth itself. The close, now incorporated within the renovated Clydesdale Bank Building in Methven Street (q.v.) is no longer recognisable. The picture was taken in 1970.

Kirk Close, 88 High Street

A through way from High Street to St John's Place and the Kirk; one of several short cuts for pedestrians travelling in a north/south direction through the town. In early times before King Edward Street and Scott Street existed the closes were an integral part of the communication system between High Street and South Street. This was almost entirely by foot. The buildings we see here have now been demolished but the close has been retained in the new building as a right of way.

Parliament Close: 77 High Street: 3rd February 1974 ▷

The close no longer exists, having been taken away when the adjacent buildings were demolished to make way for Marks & Spencer's latest store. The original Parliament Close and Parliament Hall went by the names of Bunch's Close and Bunch's House after the owner. Parliaments were held in the house, James I having eight parliaments here between 1425 and 1434. From the year 1818 the site was occupied by the Royal Arch Masonic Lodge.

Ship Inn Close, High Street

One of many neuks and crannies to be found to the rear of buildings in the old town. Not only did this passageway serve as a discreet approach to the inn but also as an entrance to the houses above, by way of the turnpike stairs.

Entrance to St Matthew's Church: winter

Snow adds decoration to the ornamental lamps at the entrance to the church. They were removed shortly after the photograph was taken. c. 1960.

Wrought Iron Window Grill

In Flesher's Vennel on the east side and about eye level this example of a blacksmith's craft may claim attention. The supremacy of the thistle over the rose and shamrock is clearly evident.

VIII. AMENITY AND MOOD

AMENITY is a word which is well understood and well used by ordinary folk whether they be men in the street or councillors in the council chamber. Many a heated discussion on preservation of amenity has taken place, and rightly so. The surroundings in which we live must be "nice".

Mood on the other hand whilst closely linked with amenity is more subtle. In the present context it can be described as a state of mind or feeling which good amenity can help to create. It has an emotional quality. Atmosphere, a third ingredient, can influence mood, either elevating or depressing it in its own peculiar way. It has to do with time of day and season of the year. Weather dominates it — wind, rain, sunshine, mist, frost, snow, rime. To photograph it to order is impossible unless the luck of a lifetime comes to your aid. The alternative is to wait, and wait. The capture of certain of the photographs to follow was through the waiting approach. Were they worth it? Do they convey that Perth has a feeling of mood about it that may be worth trying to detect? Having found it could it be considered to be part of our heritage?

Dusk on Kinnoull Hill

A sense of peace and relaxation can always be had on Kinnoull Hill on a summer evening. Views to the north, south and west seem endless. Such a place must be an asset to any city and it is Perth's good fortune to have it as part of its heritage as a place of high amenity. The hill was presented to the city as a place of recreation by Lord Dewar in 1924.

Grove of Beeches, Kinnoull Hill

Trees abound on Kinnoull Hill. There are many conifers and a wide range of hardwoods and shrubs. Mature beeches are less numerous and this grove is familiar to generations of walkers on the southern reaches of the hill.

Kinnoull Hill: surprise view

From the wooded slopes of the hill, walkers are frequently delighted by surprise views of distant landscapes.

Moods of the Riverside

The following set of seven photographs were all taken from viewpoints within a few yards of one another on the footpath on Perth Bridge. They demonstrate that although subject matter remain the same, atmosphere and mood can change the whole aspect of a scene resulting in a change in its effect on the sensitive viewer. The photograph becomes less of something that informs and more of something that satisfies: less of a record of fact and more of an appeal to the emotions. It has then ceased to be "just a photograph" and become a picture to be enjoyed.

In the following short series we have tried to capture some of the moods of the riverside which we find so appealing and which we think contribute to the Heritage of Perth.

On a bright May morning in 1953.

Midnight at full tide in September 1953.

The following winter — 1954 — the misty river reflects the weak sunlight of early afternoon.

A grey day in winter in the late 'fifties.

192

Fairy lights appear in Tay Street in the run up to Christmas, 1981 while a December day approaches its end.

A setting sun puts seal to a frosty day in January 1952.

A vignette of the scene — idealised to a degree — perhaps suggesting a vision or recall by an absent native.

195

Weeping Willows

As the River Tay ebbs and flows at "Gibraltar" (the old boat quay at the Norie-Miller Riverside Walk) the young willow shoots dip and rise.

Cricket: Australia v. Scotland: North Inch: Perth, 1972

Against a back-drop of Perth's Georgian town and with the clock in St John's Kirk standing at 5.07 p.m. the considerable crowd on the North Inch watch batsman B. C. Francis (New South Wales) face bowler E. R. Thompson (Stewart's/Melville F.P.). The non-striking batsman is K. R. Stackpole (Victoria). Other Scots, fielding, are (left to right): G. F. Goddard (Heriot's F.P.) mid off; J. R. Laing (Perthshire) gully; B. R. Hardie (Stenhousemuir and Essex) 2nd slip; H. K. More (Heriot's F.P.) 1st slip; J. Brown (Perthshire) wicket keeper; and R. Ellis (Kilmarnock) short square leg: the umpire at the bowler's end is J. M. Webster. Australia won.

Perthshire Cricket Club was founded in 1826.

Boating Pond: South Inch

Memories of happy days in the sun at the South Inch Pond are a legacy enjoyed by generations of Perth youngsters.

Widespread frost: North Inch

The sense of space on the North Inch is accentuated by the sunlight on the hoar frost. This was the scene during the severe winter in February 1982. The spire of St Matthew's stands out in the distance.

Winter strollers on the North Inch

In January and February 1982 the deep freeze was a memorable occasion in Perth. Here we see the golf course on the North Inch and, in the distance, the city spires.

Winter on the Tay near Friarton

South of Perth Harbour fog and frost are winter's recipe for a picture with atmosphere. In the distance on the left Kinnoull Hill is just visible.

Riverside ice

The ice on the bank of the Tay reflects low winter sunshine during the long freeze in the early months of 1982. Part of the golf course on the North Inch is seen on the right and in the distance, the spires of the city.

The North Inch

The Inch with its high amenity and facilities for outdoor sports and activities can on occasion be the scene of extraordinary incident. This huge bonfire, built near the foot of Barossa Place, was set alight to welcome a new prince into the world — Prince Andrew, 19th February 1960.

This picture shows the inundation of the Inch which took place at the end of January 1974 when flood-waters breached the bank of the River Almond and spread over the Inch. Here we see three schoolboys enjoying the novelty of an island perch to survey the scene.

Salmon group and fountain   ▷

The lake in Norie-Miller riverside walk contains this metal sculpture of a group of leaping salmon by Mr Scott Sutherland, D.A.(Edin.), R.S.A., F.R.B.S. The sculpture was the gift of the Quarter Century Club of the Corporation in honour of Sir Stanley. A fountain jet adds life to the scene. 1971.

Riverside Lake and Kinnoull Church   ▷

This panoramic view taken from the Norie-Miller Riverside Walk, shows Kinnoull Church and hall with, in the foreground, the lake and metal sculpture of a salmon group (q.v.). The park was laid out to honour Sir Stanley Norie-Miller, B.T., M.C., D.L., J.P., after many years of service as Chairman of the General Accident Fire Life Assurance Corporation. It was handed over to the city on behalf of the Corporation by Lord Polwarth, T.D., D.L., C.A., on 26th May 1971.

Snow etching, with geese

A skene of geese, just visible, threads its way southwards, high over the city after a November snowfall.

Sombre mood

The festive lights at Christmas time do little to dispel the approaching gloom
of a December afternoon: 1981.

Suburban Sunset ▷

Looking over the roofs of the new housing development at Corsie, on the lower slopes of Kinnoull Hill, a summer sunset is seen in the north-west.

South Inch, winter

The meagre light from this Victorian lamp standard helps but little to dispel the feeling of loneliness which can be experienced on crossing the South Inch on a winter's night. But the distant lights of Marshall Place and King Street give promise of early cheer.

Winter on Barnhill

Photograph taken in 1957 in the grounds of Barnhill Sanatorium.

Historical Note: The sanatorium was established for the treatment of tuberculosis in 1901 under the same administration as Hillside Homes. It was finally closed in 1958. The few remaining patients were then transferred to Bridge of Earn Hospital for continued treatment. The sanatorium was ideally situated, high on the hill, with southern exposure and adjacent to mixed woodland including pine of which the picture is a winter example.

Winter on the River Almond near Perth

On the northern outskirts of Perth near this spot the River Almond joins the Tay. In this picture the winter sunset adds a touch of atmosphere to the scene. The river in its course which is all within Perthshire, traverses the Sma' Glen, spills over Buchanty Spout, passes through Glenalmond, supplies mills at Ruthvenfield and Huntingtower and fills the town's lade for Perth. The lade no longer drives the city mills which it did for centuries but still runs, for the most part out of sight, through the centre of the town.

Landscape with horse

This green field site with southern exposure has been tenanted by this fortunate grey for a number of years. The scene is on the lower slopes of Kinnoull Hill and is well known to those who enjoy the hill's amenities. The hill rises to the right while on the left are the hills of Deuchney and Binn. In the distance the River Tay with the farmlands of Rhynd and Abernethy can be seen, and on the skyline the hills of Fife.

Disturbance

The River Tay, being tidal to Perth and beyond, becomes at dead water as still as a lowland loch. Our picture was taken at Kinfauns at such a time, but with it came the 'disturbance'. Was it a restless salmon or some falling object of uncertain identity?

Ardchoille Lodge, winter

Photograph taken in available street lighting. Strathmore Street, which runs across the middle of the picture, changes its usual mood of noise and bustle for a moment of quiet stillness on Christmas Eve.

IX. RIVER, ROAD AND RAIL

PERTH's origin and continued existence in the past has been dependent upon its situation at the crossing of the ways — ways by sea and river, road and rail.

The River Tay. In mediaeval times what better communication than by seagoing ship from any coastal port on the North Sea and beyond, straight to the High Street of Perth. From the harbour there, where dues would be paid, a few steps would take a merchant or sea captain to Watergate, where most of the nobility and merchant classes had a home or accommodation address, and arrangements made for the delivery of his cargo. If the ship were too big for the north shore — i.e. more than 30 tons burden — a berth could be found downstream and cargo discharged by lighter. Today the harbour is situated a mile downstream in a tidal basin. It has berths for six coasters and can accommodate ships of 250 feet long and from 400-1,200 tons dead weight. Cargoes are mainly fertiliser, timber, steel and grain. On 24th October 1981 a cargo of fertiliser weighing 1,300 tons was discharged — a record at the time. In anticipation of increasing traffic a reconstruction programme was agreed on 6th May 1983 to improve berths 1 and 2 at a cost of £70,000. Perth's Heritage as a seaport seems assured for some time to come.

The river as a resource is no less impressive. Salmon fishing has been a tradition practised since the beginnings of history. To the present-day the mention of Tay salmon has whetted many an appetite. Reference is made in this section to both industrial salmon fishing by nets and the sport by rod and line.

Another example of the river as a resource is illustrated in this section i.e. the supply of sand and gravel as raw materials for the building industry. These are dredged from the bed of the estuary and separated at the upper harbour in readiness for distribution.

Road. Perth is situated at a point on the Tay which is the upper limit of the North Sea tides — over 20 miles inland from Dundee — and where in the past the river could be crossed either by ford, ferry or when available, bridge; in other words at a junction of the ways. It was where ships could go no further and where travellers with their goods had to continue their journey overland. The word "road" as we understand it today did not apply. A footpath, bridlepath or drove road or a mixture of all three, trodden down by a process of arbitrary selection through "dub* and myre" was favoured with the name of road. Little wonder that travellers came as far as possible by boat. Scotland's introduction to "made" roads as opposed to roads as described above was by General George Wade whose military roads spread northwards at a time between the two Jacobite Rebellions of 1715 and 1745. Such was his success that the following couplet was coined:

"Had you seen these roads before they were made
You would lift up your hands and bless General Wade".

His role was later taken up by Thomas Telford and John Loudon McAdam.

---

*Dub — a deep pool in a burn.
See: Burns' *Tam o' Shanter*.

By the time John Smeaton built his notable bridge at Perth (1771) a rudimentary network of roads existed which fed on to the bridge. Then between 1750 and 1844 upwards of 350 Turnpike Roads and Bridges Acts were passed in Scotland and tolls became a normal levy. But with the arrival of later legislation and the spread of the railways their days were numbered. The Public Health Acts of 1848 and 1875 introduced local administration of roads with the result that tolls were gradually abolished.

Perth is now incorporated into a modern road network — all of the way to Edinburgh by motorway and most of the way to Glasgow and Dundee by dual carriageway. Upgrading of roads to Aberdeen and Inverness proceeds by stages.

This section shows Smeaton's Perth Bridge, the Queen's Bridge, and the more recent Friarton Bridge which link up with these arterial roadways and can now be identified with the city's ongoing heritage.

Rail. By 1848 Perth had become the meeting place of four company lines — from Dundee, Forfar, Burntisland and Glasgow, and by 1856 a line from Perth to Birnam, via Stanley Junction was completed. But the challenge of the Highlands had still to be met and under pressure from Inverness and the North the Highland Line was built (1861-63) linking Birnam with Forres. It was not until the end of the century that the more direct route to Inverness via Slochd was completed.

In 1866 a direct link from Perth to Crieff was opened and in 1906 the Perth to Bankfoot Light Railway.

Passenger traffic was mostly seasonal, particularly on the Highland Line, peaking in August; but as to livestock, in 1867 no fewer than 21,000 sheep were passing through Perth per week, in season, to lowland markets.

The axe fell in the 1950's and '60's. All branch lines in Perthshire were closed and route mileage fell from 268 in 1948 to 98 at present and stations from 78 to 11. In spite of this a useful service from Perth Station still exists on an Inter-City basis.

Looking to High Street from the east

With the spit of Stanner's Island in the foreground, the view across the River Tay leads us to the site of the old upper harbour of Perth situated exactly at the point where High Street meets the Tay. Seagoing ships could tie up here, a few minutes' walk from the business centre of the town. The present civic buildings, seen on the waterfront, occupy the site of the original harbour building where civic administration was conducted in the past.

Visit of Minesweepers of the Royal Navy to Perth

Passing Kinnoull Hill on its approach to Perth, one of the two visiting minesweepers of the Royal Navy is seen with crew mustered on deck. The lower picture shows the white minesweeper manoeuvring within the harbour. The welcome accorded the officers and men included a civic reception headed by Lord Provost John Buchan.

Sand Boat passing Friarton

On its way to the upper harbour from the estuary laden with its heavy cargo of sand and gravel.

Sand Treatment Plant

Making sand ready for use by washing and removing impurities.

Perth Harbour

This freighter gets a reception of mist and ice on a winter's visit in the 1950's. Incoming cargoes were mostly farm fertiliser and outgoing, grain, timber and occasionally potatoes. Sand and gravel were taken further upstream to the present upper harbour (q.v.).

Unloading Sand and Gravel

At the upper harbour. Note also the gasholder in the middle distance, and beyond, a part of Perth Prison (see next page).

Ray John

One of the sand boats returning fully laden with sand and gravel dredged from the estuary of the Tay.

Sand boats, Upper harbour, winter

Low temperatures combine with New Year holidays to bring all activity to a halt at the harbour. The photograph, taken in the 1950's, shows ships which are now obsolete and replaced with motor vessels. Their purpose is to dredge sand and gravel from the Tay estuary and ship it to Perth for use in the building industry. (See next page.)

Waulkmill Ferry: Stormontfield

Sandy Fraser was both the power source and the pilot on the rowing-boat ferry on the Tay at Waulkmill. Upstream from Perth it was the last surviving ferry boat between the bridges at Perth and Meikleour. The service was withdrawn in 1961.

Salmon netting at Seggieden

Toiling in the chill of winter this team could well serve as a model for a sculpture group. Seggieden is one of one of many sites on the Tay estuary where salmon netting is organised as an industry. Team is here seen drawing in after the net has been swept wide in the river. This and other forms of netting, e.g. with cruives, have been practised since the dawn of history. King Alexander II (1189-1249) introduced certain restrictions in their use. Today, by statute (viz. Salmon Fisheries (Scotland) Act 1968; and its Schedule; also Salmon and Freshwater Fisheries Protection Act, 1951) fishing for Salmon is prohibited on Sundays throughout the year. Netting is also prohibited in the close season — from 21st August to 4th February inclusive.

Angler with catch

Within an hour of paying his modest fee for a day's fishing within the city's limits this angler has landed a nice fish. Two young spectators display varying degrees of scrutiny, appraisal, approval and perhaps a little envy of his catch. Their day will come.

Rod and Line on the Tay

▷
▷

Fishing enthusiasts from all walks of life descend upon the Tay in September and early October to ply for salmon as they make their way upstream to spawn. (The season is closed from 15th October to 15th January). In the contest with the fish gamesmanship goes hand in hand with the instinct of the hunter; but in the first place a good knowledge of the river is required — the volume of flow, speed, configuration of the bed, clarity of the water, the state of the tide and not least, the weather. The River Tay is fast flowing. It conveys more water to the sea than any other river in Britain, even more than the Thames and Severn combined. Its reputation as a salmon river is among the best. The pictures show the scene near the railway bridge on an evening in September 1983.

218

Sunday rest at Seggieden

These items of equipment, inactive by law, seem to accord with the mood of the weather to produce a restful scene.

Inspection of Perth Bridge
Sophisticated techniques in use, including photography of stonework.

Victoria Bridge: demolition 1959

Constructed of steel girders on stone piers this bridge gave service from 1900 until 1959. It is here seen under demolition but its framework is still useful temporarily as a ready made staging for work on the replacement bridge — the Queen's Bridge — underneath. Huge jacks — one on each support point — raised the old steelwork to a height of 5½ feet to allow work to proceed below. One of these jacks is seen in the foreground.

Friarton Bridge from Rhynd Road

The bridge was built between 1975 and 1978. It spans the Tay south of Moncrieffe Island and links the Craigend interchange with the intersection on the Dundee road. The bridge is of box girder type, each section weighing approximately 40 tonnes, and is 831 metres long. There are two carriageways. Expansion joints allow for up to 380 mm longitudinal movement on roller bearings. The cost was approximately £8 million.

◁   ## The Queen's Bridge

Built in 1959-60 and opened by Queen Elizabeth II on 10th October 1960. It replaced the Victoria Bridge, an iron structure on stone piers, built in 1900. The bridge consists of four longitudinal beams with transverse slabs top and bottom forming three hollow boxes side by side. Prestressed on the Freyssinet system. The framework of the old bridge was raised 5½ feet on jacks to support the new structure during its construction underneath. The two pillars are built around reinforced concrete piles: 427 high tensile steel cables are incorporated. The bridge is 400 feet long and took 15 months to construct. It cost £150,000. Engineers: F. A. MacDonald & Partners. Contractors: Whatlings Ltd.

The bridge has a slender elegance which contrasts sharply with the traditional lines of Perth Bridge. (See next page.)

Friarton Bridge from Kinnoull Hill

The bridge and road complex as seen from a height of 700 feet above the river.

Perth Railway Station ▷

The facade of the exterior of the original station is shown. It now faces platform 4. Built in Tudor/Gothic style it is the work of Sir Wm. Tite of London, 1848. It now accommodates local administration and operational departments of British Rail and is beset by later additions. The Highland Line from Perth to Inverness via Forres was opened in 1863, the direct line via Slochd had to wait till the end of the century.

224

Perth Station, from St Leonard's Bridge

Looking northwards the platforms number from the right: 1-7. The Tudor type tower of the original building is prominent on the left. Listed "C". The turret with spire on the right is part of the Station Hotel. Listed "B".

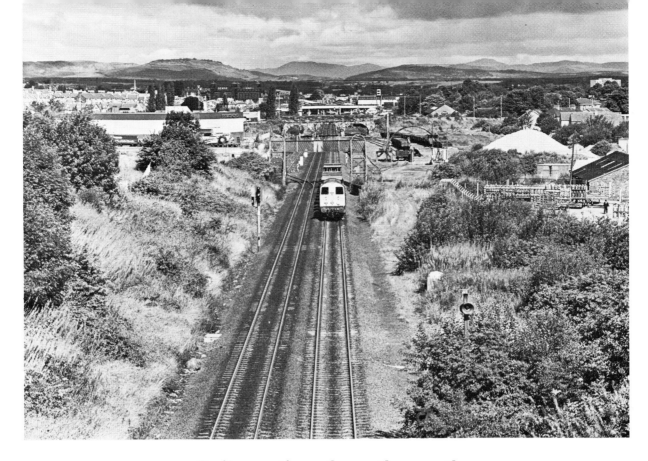

Railway lines from the south

Main lines from both Glasgow and Edinburgh join south of Perth and proceed on the lines shown. The city lies directly ahead. In the far distance, directly above the bridges, the mountains near Pitlochry can be seen. Forming part of the Grampians, the one on the left is Ben Vrackie and on the right Ben y Gloe. The wooded hills on either side of the gap are near Dunkeld.

Railway Bridge: 1955

A steam train from Dundee traverses the Moncrieffe Island on its way to Perth Station. (Steam power was replaced by diesel in the 1960's.) The island, formed by the River Tay branching into two, is the site of the King James VI golf course and a large number of garden allotments. The bridge spans both branches of the river as well as the island and replaced a wooden bridge in 1863.

"Winter Service": Perth Station 1958

These mundane words on the railway timetable are here translated into the drama of real life. A "Saturdays only", leaving platform 7 at 9.01 p.m., this train is drawn by the three-cylinder Stanier Jubilee-class locomotive "Warspite", No. 45724. It will presently be heading for Aberdeen, via Forfar, through a snow-laden north-easterly.

X.   RECENT CHANGES

IT is generally agreed that change is inevitable in a civilised society. Conversely, civic stasis, given time, invariably means civic degeneration. (If you don't look after your house, one day it will fall about your ears.) All cities at some time or other have had the experience of seeing part of their heritage crumble away through neglect and not had reasonable means to avert it. A heritage goes, never to return. Perth is no exception, but it is not my brief to raise ghosts. Heritage, like life itself, is *now,* to have and to hold and if possible improve.

Changes in the civic scene, to the man in the street, are more and more coming to mean "developments": shopping developments, housing developments, business developments, industrial developments, sports developments. Occasionally however, a fine old building is restored or a block of Victorian flats is refurbished but these are exceptions.

At this point attention is drawn to three outstanding examples of restoration projects in Perth which have undoubtedly enhanced our civic heritage. The first is the old waterworks building in Marshall Place which was restored in 1973-74 and now houses the Fergusson Art Gallery, and the second is the King James VI Hospital, restored 1973–75. The third is the city mills buildings involving both upper and lower mills. The former was preserved successfully and converted to use as a hotel and the latter has been restored to full mill status. All three of these projects concern buildings listed in the "A" category and have been illustrated in section I. Yet another building in this category — the Old Academy (q.v), Rose Terrace — has been restored (1996) and is now used as office accommodation.

In the following pages which form our final section; some examples of recent changes are shown. All are in the fields of housing and business. As to whether any of the new buildings will earn a high place in Perth's Architectural Heritage is for time to tell. We look to the future.

General Accident Assurance Corporation: Perth Agency Office

Situated in South St John's Place this new building sits in juxtaposition with St John's Kirk, south transept, whose mullioned window appears in reflection. Note the device of the corporation.

Pickembrae, Pitheavlis

A country walk could be enjoyed in October 1980 near the site of building works on the office complex of the General Accident Fire Life Assurance Corporation at Pitheavlis. Completed and occupied in 1983 the visual effect on the countryside by the complex has been surprisingly slight.

Clydesdale Bank Development: South Methven Street   ▷

The accompanying four photographs give at a glance the train of events during 1979-81 at Nos. 23-31 South Methven Street. The earliest one, taken in August 1979 shows the original bank building — Victorian Renaissance of 1888 which is shortly described as two-storeyed with pedimented Ionic corner entrance and doorpiece, and with first-floor panel and sculptured spandrels. There are two large and one small window bays to Methven Street. It is listed "B". Beyond this building, northwards in Methven Street stands the Central Motor Garage. Comparing this with photograph of November 1981 the new bank building occupies the site of Central Motor Garage. The remaining two photographs show the rear aspect of the building from different angles. This faces into Mill Wynd. The old gable of "Hal o' the Wynd's House" with its Flemish influence is given a prominent presence in the facade which otherwise is traditional Scottish domestic. These older styles are not in any way upset by the modern lines of the new windows at the back of the bank which are stood back deferentially. Messrs McCash & Hunter, solicitors, share the new building with the bank. (See next two pages.)

Clydesdale Bank before development as seen from the south.

Clydesdale Bank after development as seen from the north.

Above and below: Clydesdale Bank development, face to Mill Wynd from different angles showing Hal o' the Wynd's House.

Spey Court: Canal Street

This small group of artisan's houses was erected by Mr A. K. Bell, whisky distiller and blender, in the year 1920. The site had become vacant following a fire in one of his bonded stores. Recently repainted, Spey Court has taken on a new look. Old militia barracks (Victoria Buildings) situated on a site to the right survived until 1982, having been used for a time as housing.

Former General Post Office

This photograph, taken in September 1973 just before its demolition, shows the impressive building in its central situation in the city at the corner of High Street with Scott Street. Designed by Walter Wood Robertson of the Edinburgh Office of Works for the Postmaster General's Department, it was Perth's third G.P.O. having been opened on 27th June 1898 to replace the second which was situated at the corner of High Street and Tay Street and which had been in use since 1862. The first post office was at the corner of George Street and Charlotte Street (q.v.). The building shown was taken down after the completion of the present G.P.O. in South Street.

◁   ## Playhouse Cinema, Murray Street.

One of few art-deco buildings in Perth; erected in the nineteen thirties. Listed "B" in 1991, when photographed.

Corner block: High Street/Scott Street

This photograph, taken in 1983, shows the building which replaced the former General Post Office seen in adjoining photograph. It has accommodation for shops and offices.

High Street: Nos. 86-102

Built about 1770-80, this block of domestic buildings had an eyecatching quaintness among the neighbouring Victorian buildings. This attractive feature is now lost as the result of recent (1980) total plastering. It was described as four-storey, rubble built, with ground floor shops and Gothic detail at centres of third floors. Was listed "B".

Moir's Buildings, St Catherine's Road

Now demolished, this building was situated at the corner of St Catherine's Road and West High Street. It was a handsome building although not listed. Relief sculptures of Wheel and the City Arms were situated high on the building and are to be seen, enlarged, on the adjoining photographs. An ancient chapel of St Catherine which was attached to the Carmelite Priory of Tullilum was situated near the spot and explains the name of the road and the emblem of the Wheel which was associated with her martyrdom. Moir's Buildings were erected by a baillie, James Moir, a mason and builder whose yard was nearby. He was R.W.M. of Masonic Lodge Scoon & Perth No. 3 from 1878-81. The corner shop was occupied by his son Alexander, a licensed grocer, but in its latter days it was the premises of a chain saw specialist. A block of modern flats was built on the site in 1993.

Old houses: Nos. 1-25 Strathmore Street

Part of this block of old houses is shown, taken shortly before demolition to make way for the new flats shown in the adjoining photographs.

Council flats: Nos. 75-109 Main Street, Bridgend

Were erected in 1970 on the same site as the old houses on the adjoining photograph which were demolished in 1968. The flats are pleasantly situated as they overlook the Bell Park from which this photograph was taken. They are also convenient to shops but the noise of traffic is almost continuous.

Council flats: Nos. 75-109 Main Street, Bridgend

Another view of the new flats erected in 1970. The Bell Park is shown on the left.

◁ *Cleared area at junction of Meal Vennel with South Street*

Taken from a viewpoint to the rear of Scott Street the sites of the future G.P.O. and Royal Bank of Scotland are seen as temporary car parks in 1959. The stone sets of the old vennel are clearly visible. On the right, part of the south side of South Street, in shadow, containing Reliance Motors became Tesco's first supermarket in Perth.

"New" city centre after completion (1962)

General view from the same spot as above sometime after completion of the centre. In 1984 plans for a large shopping mall in its place were under construction, and became reality in 1987.

◁ ## "New" city centre under construction (1959)

Building in progress as seen from a flat in Scott Street. The old paving of Meal Vennel is seen in the immediate foreground, also the spires of St John's (right) and St Matthew's Churches.

R

Strathmore Street, Bridgend: old and new

Old Strathmore Street, photographed in January 1972, began to grow following the building of Perth Bridge (1771). The landlord was the Earl of Kinnoull. It was demolished 1973.

New Strathmore Street (below) photographed in September 1980 from the same viewpoint, shows the new sheltered housing. Key to the comparison is the stone gatepost seen on the right of both pictures.

Potterhill Flats under construction 1960

Tower blocks for housing were wisely rejected by Perth City Council in the '50's and '60's. Medium rise flats such as at Potterhill met the needs of the time but on this particular site were not received with universal acclaim.

Park, Leonard Street, 1958

In 1958 these three smiling schoolboys sat unaware and probably unconcerned that the church on their left would within a year be levelled to the ground and with it the nearby tenement. Two years later (1960) the Pomarium flats would be built in their place and ready for occupation. The church was St Stephen's.

Demolition at Pomarium Street

In 1959 the old houses in Pomarium Street were demolished to make way for the new blocks of flats to be built under the council's housing programme. Here we see one of the old houses partly demolished and in the background construction work proceeding on the new flats.

The street derived its name from the orchard or pomarium belonging to the monks of the Carthusian Monastery sited nearby, and which was destroyed after the Reformation (1559).

Pomarium Flats under construction 1959

A photograph taken from an attic window of one of the old flats in Pomarium Street which was under demolition at the time. The new construction is in progress and was completed in 1960. Built to the general standards in vogue at the time, the new flats compare with many others erected throughout the country and which can be seen today in various states of preservation. We cannot fairly expect them to contribute any significant part to the proud heritage of Perth, but that the name "Pomarium" with its historic connections survives is to be acknowledged.

246

Part of Bridgend from the North Inch

Highlighted in the centre of the riverside houses is Bridgend Court. This, along with the smaller houses stepping down to the river, was built by Keystone Development in 1972-73. A successful blend of old with new has been achieved. The house seen on extreme left — "Newlands" — is listed "B".

Old Commercial Street: from Perth Bridge

Smoking chimneys tell their tale of afternoon fires being made up for tea time. The year was 1963 but 11 more years were to pass before any material change was to take place in this scene. The old street which ran parallel to the river just behind the row of riverside buildings, dated from before the building of Perth Bridge — 1771. The lowest part led into a slipway used by ferry boats. This point also corresponded with the eastern end of a mediaeval bridge built by John Mylne in the reign of James VI and which at its western end was continuous with High Street. It was swept away in 1621. The inhabitants of the Commercial Street area — a ferry village in fact — were in great part river orientated, viz. ferrymen, boatmen, sailors, wharf workers. There were importers of wine, maltsters, brewers, bakers. Sixteen taverns were scattered around the Bridgend area; most notable of those, the Cross Keys (q.v.) where the owner, Mr Clark, supplied not only food and shelter but horses and transport to Coupar Angus, Dundee and the east. The name Clark survived until 1975 in "Clark's Close", a narrow passage running from Commercial Street to the river and which can be seen on the photograph, near the centre. The whole of this riverside area was demolished in 1975. The new Commercial Street (q.v.) was built on the same site.

Old Commercial Street from south

As seen from Queen's Bridge the houses are thrown into relief by morning sunshine. The trees of the garden of old Ferry House (right) and of Stanner's Island (left) frame the scene. Demolition took place in 1975.

Stages in the Clearance of Old Commercial Street

Above, the half-way stage and below, total clearance (1975-76). Near the centre of the lower picture houses of the new scheme are already being erected on the site. Kinnoull Church can be seen on the extreme right, while on the extreme left, 'Glenshaugh', Gowrie Street.

Building a Groyne in the Tay

A mechanised digger takes the advantage of low water to lay a groyne between Perth Bridge and Stanner's Island. The desired effect of diverting part of the river water to the east of the island was achieved, thereby improving amenity and sanitation. In the background finishing touches are being made to the houses. Photo: August 1977.

Variety in housing

The photograph shows how a low-rise development — the new Commercial Street — can sit comfortably with a block of eight levels — Potterhill flats — in close proximity.

New Commercial Street

The scheme, now completed (1978) as seen from two different viewpoints — above, from the N.W. on Perth bridge and, below, from the south.

Built on the site of the old street in the years 1976-78 this group of council houses can claim to be part of Perth's Heritage in the making. Each generation makes its own imprint to be passed on. This development was considered outstanding enough to qualify for awards from the Civic Trust and other bodies (q.v.). The architects were Messrs Parr, Broughty Ferry, Dundee.

Commercial Street: The new development from the south

From a viewpoint at the site of the old ferry slip, the proximity of the new houses to the river is clearly seen. Echoing the design of the little houses (1976) recently demolished on the same site, the balconies reach out over the river. This attractive feature with the good planning standards otherwise exhibited go a long way to match the exceptionally fine qualities of the site. The advice of the Perth Civic Trust was freely given at the planning stages. The architects were James Parr and partners, Dundee with builders McAdam, Perth. The development won various awards, as follows: — a Civic Trust Award; a Perth Civic Trust Award; a Saltire Award; an R.I.B.A. Commendation; a certificate from the Scottish Concrete Society; and from the European Cement Association; a commendation from the Institute Nationale D'Logements; Prix International d'Architecture of the Belgian Housing Association, an Ambrose Congreve Commendation and a Cembureau Award.

Index

Academy: 14 - 17
Agnus Dei Symbol: 42
Albert Close: 176
Alexandra Street: 175
Almond, River: 206
Annat Lodge: 107
Ardchoille House: 101
Ardchoille Lodge: 208
Art Gallery, *See* Museum
Atholl Crescent: 17, 18, 55
Atholl Place: 19
Atholl Crescent: 17, 18
Atholl Street: 80, 149

Bakers Guild: 7
Balhousie Castle: 70
Bank of Scotland: 39
Barnhill Sanatorium: 205
Barnhill Tollhouse: 36, 37
Barossa Place: 58
Bell, Arthur Kinmond: 234
Bell, King James VI Hospital: 32
Bell Park: 239
Bell, A K, Library (Old Infirmary): 41
Bells, St. Johns: 10
Bell's Sports Centre: 96
Bellwood House: 111
Boating Pond: 197
"Boatland": 106
Bowerswell House: 104
Bowerswell Road: 114
Bridgend: 234, 239, 242, 247

Caledonian Road: 173
Caller Fountain Hill: 160
Candelabrum: 5
Canal Crescent: 144
Canal Street: 164, 165, 234
Carving: 6 - 8
Cavendish Avenue: 155
Charlotte Place: 33
Charlotte Street: 33, 153
Charlotte Street - West Side: 51
Charlotte Street - East Side: 53
Charlotte Street - No. 6: 54
Churches - *See* Under Individual Names e.g.
    St. Matthews Church:
City Centre: 240, 241
City Hall: 71
City Mills: 20, 21
Clydesdale Bank: 231 - 233
Commercial Street: 155, 248 - 250, 253, 254
Congregational Church: 84
Cordiners Guild: 6
County Buildings: 40
County Place: 141
Craigie Hill: 160
Craigie Park House: 100
Craigie Road: 100
Curfew Row: 97

District Council Building: 60 - 67, 69

Do'cot Park: 108
Dundee Road: 111

East Bridge Street: 154
Employment Exchange: 175

Fair Maid's House: 97
Flesher's Building: 175
Flesher's Guild: 7
Flesher's Vennel: 183
Flood: 200
Foundry: 171
Fountain Close: 179
Friarton: 213
Friarton Bridge: 223, 224

General Accident Assurance: 230
General Accident Building *See* District Council
    Building
George Street: 51, 52, 90, 117 - 119, 177:
Glasgow Road: 105
"Glenshaugh": 114
Glover's Guild: 6
Glover's Hall: 177
Greyfriars Burial Ground: 78, 79
Guilds: 6, 7

Hal o' The Wynd's Close: 179
Hal o' The Wynd's House: 233
Hamilton House: 105
Hammermen Guild: 4, 6
Harbour: 212, 214, 216
Hay, George, 11th Earl of Kinnoull: 76
High Street: 49, 61, 63, 120, 121, 123 - 125,
    127 - 131, 134, 135, 178, 182, 211,
    236, 237
High Street, No. 13: 50
High Street, No. 9-11: 116
High Street Port: 136
Honeyman, John: 68

Infirmary, Old: 41
Isla Road: 101, 106

Kincarrathie Do'cot: 109
Kincarrathie House: 108
Kincarrathie House Chapel: 109
Kinfauns Castle: 161, 162
King Edward Street: 71, 126
King James VI Hospital: 28 - 30, 32
King James VI Hospital, Interior: 31
King's Place, No. 6: 112
Kinnoull Church: 72, 74, 75, 77, 201
Kinnoull Church, Interior: 73
Kinnoull Hill: 162, 186 - 188
Kinnoull Street: 84, 132, 135
Kirk Close: 180
Knox, Robert, boatman: 77
Kirkgate: 158
Kirkton Hill: 160

Lade: 21, 137

Leonard Street, Park: 244
Lochie Brae: 154

McKenzie, W M: 41
Main Street: 239
Marshall Monument: 52, 88, 90
Marshall Place: 34
Marshall, Thomas Hay: 46, 47, 91
Mary Cup: 4
Meal Vennel: 241
Melville Street: 58
Melville Street, No. 26: 114
Mercat Cross: 126
Mercers of Aldie: 49
Middle Church: 83
Mill Street: 133, 137
Mill Wynd: 179, 233
Mills: 20, 21
Moir's Buildings: 238
Moncrieffe Island: 226
Muirhall Road: 85
Murray Royal Hospital : 85 - 87
Murray Royal Hospital Chapel: 86, 87
Murray Street: 137
Museum: 88, 92
Mylne, John, Master Mason: 79

Needless Road: 38
"Newlands": 247
Norie-Miller Riverside Walk: 201
North Church: 81
North Inch: 55, 153, 197, 198, 200
North St. John's Place: 144
Northern District School: 94

Offerand Stok of St. Eloyi: 4
Old High Street: 134
Old Presbytery: 114

Parliament Close: 181
Perth Bridge, See Smeaton, John, Bridge
Pickembrae: 231
Pitheavlis: 231
Pitheavlis Castle: 38
Playhouse Cinema: 234
Pomarium Flats: 245, 246
Post Office: 132, 235
Post Office, Old: 90
Potterhill Flats: 243, 252
Princes Street: 157
Prison: 95
Prudential Assurance: 49
Pullar & Sons Ltd: 133

Queen's Bridge: 152, 222

Railway Bridge: 11, 226
Rattray's Tobacconist: 130
Reform Place: 164
Reid, Robert: 17
Ropemaker's Close: 174
Rose Terrace: 14 - 17, 55
Rose Terrace, Provost Marshall's House: 47

St. Catherine's Road: 238
St. John's Kirk Interior: 9
St. John's Kirk: 2, 3, 43, 230
St. John's Street: 39, 122
St. Leonard's Bank, No. 10: 110
St. Leonard's Church, King Street: 82
St. Leonard's in the Fields Church: 34, 35, 160
St. Magdalene's Road: 113
St Matthew's Church: 60, 67 - 69, 159, 183, 202
St. Matthew's Hall: 170
St. Ninian's Cathedral: 80
St. Paul's Church: 136
St. Stephen's Church: 244
Salutation Hotel: 49
Sand Boats: 213, 215, 216
Sand Treatment Plant: 213
Sandeman Library: 81, 84
Scott, Sir Walter, statue: 34
Scott Street: 133
Seggieden: 217, 220
Sharp's Institution: 93
Ship Inn Close: 182
Shoemakers Guild: 6
Smeaton, John, bridge: 10, 12, 13, 51, 156, 221
South Esk Bank: 113
South Inch: 197, 204
South Methven Street: 93, 138 - 140, 231
South St. John's Place: 230
South Street: 48, 142, 143, 145, 146, 172 - 175, 179
South Street Port: 140, 143
Spey Court: 234
Springland: 101 - 103
Stanners Island: 251
Station: 225, 227
Stormontfield: 217
Strathmore Street: 101, 239, 242

Tailor's Guild: 8
Tay, River: 152, 189 - 196, 199, 207, 218, 219, 251
Tay Street: 40, 52, 60 - 62, 67, 147, 148, 152, 202, 203
Toll House: 36, 37

Victoria Bridge: 222
Viewlands House: 110
Viewlands Road: 110

Watergate, No's 3 & 5: 49, 166, 167
Waterworks: 22 - 27
Waulkmill Ferry: 217
Weavers Guild: 7
Window, late 18th century: 178
Wright's Guild: 7
Wright's Hall: 168, 169
Wright's Incorporation: 166, 167

York Place: 41
Youth Hostel: 105